THE BOY SCOUT COUNCIL SHOULDER PATCH GUIDE

A Tour of Councils Through Their Patches

VOLUME FOUR

STEVEN AND ELISA DELMAN

S & E PUBLISHING COMPANY

POMONA, NEW YORK

THE BOY SCOUT COUNCIL SHOULDER PATCH GUIDE

• • • • •

This compendium is not an official or authorized publication of the Boy Scouts of America. The information contained herein was assembled from discussions with more than 350 Scouters acting in their individual capacities and not as officials of the BSA or any Council thereof.

An outline of the material was presented to and discussed with legal counsel for the BSA and publication is without objection by the BSA following prior disclosure of format, sample content and plans for distribution.

No claim is made to the copyright in any BSA or Council patch, image or mark. However, copyright is claimed as to the assembly, organization and text presented in this publication.

• • • • •

1st Printing July 2000

Printed in the United States of America

International Standard Serial Number: 1099-436X

ISBN: 0-9657239-4-1

Manufactured in the United States of America

Published by:
S & E PUBLISHING COMPANY
5 Beaver Dam Road
Pomona, New York 10970
845-362-1800
Fax: 845-362-3252
E-mail: sd@scoutpatch.com

Volume Four

TABLE OF CONTENTS

ACKNOWLEDGEMENTS

We would once again like to thank our many readers for making the Third Edition a success and for your wonderful comments, letters, e-mails, faxes, and phone calls. Your input has helped us to continually improve, expand and enrich each volume.

A special thanks to all those who have volunteered to be Council Patch Watchers. Our Council Patch Watchers have kept us abreast of new patches and supplied us with invaluable insights and information.

This book, like many Scouting projects, is the result of the combined efforts of many volunteers. To all the individuals from the many Councils who provided information, we want you to know that your efforts are greatly appreciated. In some cases, your information appears in this book with little or no modifications. We hope that you enjoy seeing your contributions. Thank you to all those unnamed individuals.

We would especially like to thank all the Councils for their help and generosity in providing their millennium and 90th anniversary patches to us.

A special thanks to Steve Austin, CSP expert and author of the column, "The CSP Corner" for allowing us to borrow his patches and pick his brain. His quarterly articles may be read in *The American Scouting Traders Association Report*.

Many thanks to Jean Fuller, our friend and editor, for the countless hours she spent reviewing the guide and for working through many lunch hours to meet our deadline.

Much appreciation to our son and Eagle Scout, Gregg, for his contributions, unique perspective, and for getting us started in both the Scouting program and patch collecting. Without him, there would be no book.

Lastly, thanks to our friends and family, such as Robyn Small, John Damtoft, Peter Liter and our daughter Kim, who helped and encouraged us throughout this project.

CONFESSIONS OF A PATCH COLLECTOR

I was first introduced to patch collecting by an older Scout in my troop. We had a tradition of setting aside one Troop meeting a year as hobby night. After four Scouts talked about the usual hobbies of stamp collecting, baseball card collecting, jigsaw puzzle building and such, the older Scout brought out a bag of Council Shoulder Patches, or CSPs. He had recently returned from the 1989 National Jamboree, where he had learned about patch collecting. He sat there and showed off his patches. Each one was unique. Each one told a story. Western Alaska Council and Maui Council were his prize patches. After the meeting, he let us look through his patches and explore the images on them. I was intrigued. I did not understand the stories they were telling, but I knew that I would become a patch collector, nonetheless.

After that initial encounter with CSPs, I went to the local BSA distributor and purchased the patches available from the Councils in my area. I was surprised to learn that I could get patches from other BSA Councils there as well. After picking up those patches, I headed off to a four-Council Camporee and a Patch-O-Ree run by my Council and started trading patches. I then showed my friends and relatives the patches I had collected, and I started receiving patches as gifts. My little collection slowly, but surely, started to grow. Of course, I did not get the full impact of patch collecting until I went to the 1993 National Jamboree. I did more collecting there than I had ever thought imaginable. The Jamboree is a wild time for patch collectors.

However, I was still left in the dark as to the significance of these patches. What were these symbols? What stories were they trying to tell? Why did they put these images on this patch? This curiosity was not just with "foreign" Councils; it was with my own Council as well. I was from Rockland County Council, and our patch had on it a man with a tricorn hat. No one knew who this person was. I believed he was Henry Hudson because he wrote favorably in his logs about our part of the Hudson River. He even mentioned that the Hook Mountain region, located in our Council, was his favorite area along the Hudson River. I later found out that I was totally wrong. The picture of the man in the tricorn hat is a caricature of Rocky Bull, an American Revolutionary War figure.

Every part of the Boy Scout uniform has its purpose. Nothing is just what it seems to be. The belt can become a fishing line, and the neckerchief can be used as a cravat. The CSPs too are chameleons. They are our Councils' history lessons, and they express pride in our local regions and in our nation. So, as you read through this book, I invite you to take a journey through the Councils, through the homesteads of America, and through time and history as well.

MORE CONFESSIONS

Patch swapping is as old as Boy Scouts. It started as a way to encourage boys to overcome their shyness and make new friends. A patch is swapped as a token gift, and then the swappers usually exchange tales of what they have done, what their troops did, about the places they live, and other hobbies they enjoy. It is not uncommon for the adults to do the same. Sharing our ideas with other Scouts and Scouters can teach us new ways to enrich our troop's Scouting program or maybe teach us a trick to make our job go more smoothly.

Jamborees are the mecca for patch swappers. The problem with patch swapping is that sometimes, somewhere in the hunt for dinosaurs, aliens, and that untouchable Yoda, we may lose sight of the true objective: making new friends. This is easy when we get so lost in patch collecting that we do not take the time to communicate with one another. Unfortunately, many of us have fallen into this trap.

It was not until the 1997 Jamboree that I realized that sometimes it is more fun to memorize all the faces of the people I traded with, rather than just focusing on the designs of their patches. Certainly, there is a thrill in obtaining the last patch of a 14-patch set; but at the same time if that is all you do, then you are missing out on the friends along the way. I believe that is the true difference between patch swapping and patch trading.

REFLECTIONS OF A PATCH COLLECTOR

This year the BSA is celebrating two magnificent milestones. Scouting has turned a young ninety years old and, like the rest of the western world, the BSA is celebrating the year 2000. In the back of this book, you will be able to check out the patches that commemorate the 90th anniversary of BSA as well as specially designed millennium patches. They are not only for wearing on the uniform, but are also a special reminder of the history and progress of Scouting. That's why they are included in this volume.

Sharing adventures, telling stories and spending time with others is what Scouting is all about. These elements are integral to both Scouting and life itself. I find it amazing that we have such great experiences through Scouting. In the past 90 years, the BSA has trained America's boys and created today's men. The BSA has commemorated and challenged Scouts during 14 Jamborees. Next year will be the 15th Jamboree, and the first one of the new millennium. The future of Scouting has never looked better; we have good reason to celebrate. In the end, swapping patches is just a great little bonus.

I am looking forward to seeing all of you in the future, hopefully at the National Jamboree; so keep an extra patch ready so we can swap, ok?

Greggory Ian Delman

COUNCIL SHOULDER PATCHES: THE FOLK ART OF THE COUNCILS

Folk art is defined as an art form, such as carving, needlework, painting, drawing, pottery, embroidered pictures, furniture making, or quilting, created by artists or artisans with no formal academic art training. Folk artists are ordinary people who have designed their works for the general public, not for a museum or an affluent collector. Often times, the art is passed down from generation to generation through practicing artists or artisans. The tradition continues in its style, technique, and form. Much of folk art is also representative of a specific group. For example, the Amish are famous for their barn signs, painted chests, and quilts; whalers are crafters of scrimshaw—carvings on whalebone, ivory, or wood. Another attribute that sets folk art apart is that the art form is utilitarian as well as decorative.

Under this definition, each Council's patch is actually a replica of an original work of folk art. The artists that have designed the prototype for each of these patches have continued a tradition that dates back to April 1970 when the first creative CSP was authorized for uniform wear. Prior to this, red and white Council Strips were worn to designate a Scout's home council. Each Council's artist has expressed himself based on what he feels are the important highlights found within his Council. He has mixed the functionality of an identification badge with the beauty of a work of art. He has told his story in a simple, straightforward manner. The multicolored patches give us glimpses into the very fiber of each Council's make up. We learn bits of the Council's history, their environment, and even their personality via their Council Shoulder Patches.

So next time you glance at the many patches you have collected, take a minute to appreciate each patch's intricacies and beauty, for they truly are the folk art of the Councils.

PREFACE

Our search for patches has led us to travel throughout the country. We have personally gathered patches from as far away as Alaska, Hawaii and the Virgin Islands. Our recreational vehicle seems to have a Scouting homing device. There we are, traveling down a road, we make a wrong turn, and magically end up on Boy Scout Way. We can not tell you how many times this has happened to us. This CSP Guide appears to be our destiny.

Our family's Scouting adventures began when Elisa became a Cub Scout Den Leader for our son, Gregg. Later, when Gregg crossed over into Boy Scouting, Steve became an Assistant Scoutmaster and then Scoutmaster. We are now active as merit badge counselors and members of our Troop Committee.

During our years in Scouting, Gregg developed a contagious interest in patch collecting. At first, we simply purchased or traded patches that appealed to us. The more patches we collected, the more curious we became about the stories represented on each Council's Shoulder Patch (CSP). This curiosity has inspired us to learn more about the CSPs we collected. We thought others might be curious as well. We have written this book to share what we have learned with other Scouts, Scouters, and anyone else who might share our interest.

What is this book about? Just as no two Council patches are the same, neither is the information we collected about each Council. In some cases, it is the story depicted on the CSP. In others, it is about significant areas, buildings, landmarks, people, or historical events that took place within the Council's borders. Whether the CSP traveled into space aboard the Space Shuttle or Walt Disney designed a feature of the patch, each Council has something that makes it special and unique. We have tried to find these special facts to share them with you. This book presents short descriptions and does not have the room to delve into complete details. If you would like to learn more about a person, event, place or Council, then we have accomplished our goal. We encourage you to visit your library or go on-line to expand your knowledge.

This book is also a color catalog of CSPs now in use. We attempted to include CSPs current through June 30, 2000. The Councils also issue Special Activity Patches (SAPs) to commemorate anniversaries and other special events or activities, such as a Philmont trek or a Friends of Scouting contribution. These patches have the same shape as Council Shoulder Patches. It is our policy to publish the patch the Council tells us is the standard CSP. This year's volume of the guide also includes patches that Commemorate Scouting's 90th Anniversary and the new millennium. These SAPs are not accompanied by descriptions for lack of space. It is also our practice to retire both patches that have changed and patches from Councils that have merged since our last volume.

All information is correct to the best of our knowledge. We have provided information about the symbolism and the designer of each patch, where available. This information was obtained from the Council itself, the Council historian, the patch designer, or a knowledgeable Council Scouter. We would appreciate your help in keeping us informed of any changes and additional information you might have. You can contact us via the U.S. Postal Service, fax, or at our e-mail address listed on page 116. Even better, become a Council Patch Watcher and let us know when your Council changes its patch.

We hope you enjoy this book and that the explanations and descriptions, along with the image of each patch, will allow you, whether you are a casual or an avid collector, the enjoyment of "having" all of the Council patches and provide you with the opportunity to enrich your knowledge.

Steve and Elisa Delman
Revised July 2000

How to Use this Guide

We have organized this book alphabetically by the state in which the Council's office is located, and then alphabetically by Councils within that state. At the top of each page, you will find a heading listing the states on that page. Each Council has an **information** line, a **description**, and a **Scout** line. At the back of the book you will find an Index that lists the Councils alphabetically; Council Information pages with telephone numbers, addresses, and websites; and an OA Lodge Index.

A sample format of a typical page and an explanation follows:

CSP Update Abbreviations ⟶ N, V, B, A, M

N	=	New CSP Design.
B	=	Back to former design
V	=	Small design variation.
A	=	90th Anniversary SAP see Council index.
M	=	Millennium SAP see Council index.

HUDSON VALLEY Salisbury Mills, NY **Type** U **Issue** '99 **OA** Nacha Nimat #86
Description: Hudson Valley Council was formed .... (see page 49)

Scout_____ Date _____ Tel_____ E-mail _____

HUDSON VALLEY	=	Council's name
Salisbury	=	Council's city
NY	=	Council's state
Type	=	Type of patch availability (U, R, N)
U	=	Unrestricted, available from the Council and BSA National
R	=	Restricted, sold at the Council, and possibly at local stores
N	=	Non-BSA, sold at the Council, and possibly at local stores. The BSA does not manufacture these patches.
Issue	=	Date patch was first issued
'99	=	1999, or ____ date unknown
OA	=	Order of the Arrow
Tribe	=	Tribe of the Mic-O-Say
Nacha Nimat #86	=	The Council's OA Lodge name and number
Scout	=	This line is included for you to record trade information. We hope this encourages you to keep in contact with the new friends you make. Record the name of the Scout you acquired the CSP from here.
		Use the additional spaces to record:
Date	=	Trade or acquired date.
Tel	=	Telephone number.
E-mail	=	e-mail address.

Commonly Used Abbreviations

BSA	=	Boy Scouts of America
CSP	=	Council Shoulder Patch
SAP	=	Special Activity Patch

M

ALABAMA-FLORIDA Dothan, AL **Type** U **Issue** 7/97 **OA** Cowikee #224
Description: This patch was the winning design submitted by Joey Graddy, a Scout in Hartford, Alabama, Troop 32. The helicopter represents U.S. Army Aviation Base Fort Rucker and the U.S. Army Aviation Museum. The peanut denotes that the area is a large peanut growing region. The flags pictured are the State Flags of Alabama and Florida, respectively. The Council covers eight counties in southeast Alabama and two in northwest Florida. Floating in the clouds is the number "3," the Council's number. The blue water and waterfowl symbolize the Chattahoochee River and the area's many birds.
Scout_____ Date _____ Tel_____ E-mail _____

BLACK WARRIOR Tuscaloosa, AL **Type** N **Issue** ____ **OA** Aracoma #481
Description: This Council is named in honor of the Choctaw leader Tuscaloosa, or "Black Warrior." Tuscaloosa was defeated in battle by Hernando de Soto in 1540. In this bloody battle, 2,500 Native Americans were killed or died by their own hands rather than come under Spanish rule. Only 20 Spaniards were killed. The Black Warrior River, which flows through the Council's territory, is also named for him. A Native American giving the Scout Sign is shown in the center of the CSP representing the area's Native American heritage. The Council's home city was once a village inhabited by the Creek tribe. Also depicted is the Council's geographical position within the state of Alabama. The deer and turkey are symbolic of the area's abundant wildlife.
Scout_____ Date _____ Tel_____ E-mail _____

GREATER ALABAMA Birmingham, AL **Type** R **Issue** '98 **OA** Cossa #50
Description: This Council was formed is a result of the merger of the former Central Alabama, Choccolocco, and Tennessee Valley Councils. The new Council has retained the Choccolocco Council designation number, "1." The patch proudly features this number superimposed on the Scouting fleur-de-lis. The three golden sunrays, each emblazoned with a cream-colored star, symbolize the three merged Councils. Also pictured are two Scouts gazing outward, looking towards the new Council's future.
Scout_____ Date _____ Tel_____ E-mail _____

MOBILE AREA Mobile, AL **Type** U **Issue** ____ **OA** Woa Cholena #322
Description: This Council's area includes Alabama's only seaport and one of the country's busiest since the 1700's. The seaport's economic and strategic location was recognized even by early settlers. This has led six governments to rule over Mobile, giving the area the nickname, "City of Six Flags." These six flags and governments are represented on the CSP from left to right: France (1702), Great Britain (1763), United States of America (1819), Confederate States of America (1860), Spain (1780), and the Republic of Alabama (1817).
Scout_____ Date _____ Tel_____ E-mail _____

M

 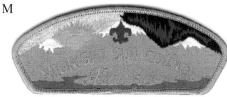

TUKABATCHEE AREA Montgomery, AL **Type** R **Issue** '87 **OA** Alabama #179
Description: Tukabatchee is the name of the Indian chief of the Alibamu Indians, a branch
of the Creek. The "Heart of Dixie" is featured within the shape of the state of Alabama. The
BSA fleur-de-lis centered in the Heart of Dixie represents Alabama's love of Scouting. The
14 stars on the patch stand for the 14 counties served by the Council. In 1955, Martin Luther
King, Jr. led a yearlong boycott of Montgomery's segregated bus system. This was one of
the first major successes of the Civil Rights Movement. The Civil Rights Memorial, which
honors 40 people who died for their beliefs of racial equality, is found in this capitol city.
Scout_____ Date _____ Tel_____ E-mail _____

MIDNIGHT SUN Fairbanks, AK **Type** R **Issue** '80s **OA** Toontuk #549
Description: This Council is suitably named for the 24 hours of daylight known as the "midnight sun." The midnight sun, which appears from mid-May until mid-July, is represented
on the patch by the golden-yellow sun. The red patterns (top right) represent another astronomical phenomenon, the "northern lights" or "aurora borealis." These are visible on many
dark Alaskan nights. The three mountains are the Debra, Hess, and Kayes, which are all part
of the Alaska Range. The green area at the foot of the mountain depicts the Tanana Flats, a
part of the Alaskan Tundra. The brown Tanana River flows through the green tundra.
Scout_____ Date _____ Tel_____ E-mail _____

SOUTHEAST ALASKA Juneau, AK **Type** R **Issue** '84 **OA** Kootz #523
Description: The yellow background represents the sun. On the totem pole is a Kootz or
brown bear. "Grizzly," the CSP's Kootz, is the Council's totem. The Council is home to the
world's largest brown bear population. The Alaska state flag is shown indicting the Council's state capital location. Appearing on the flag are the Big Dipper (Ursa Major—the Great
Bear) and the North Star (Polaris). The Council is a maritime Council situated on islands
that are sea bound, accessible only by water or air.
Scout_____ Date _____ Tel_____ E-mail _____

WESTERN ALASKA Anchorage, AK **Type** U **Issue** '92 **OA** Nanuk #355
Description: This patch typifies the abundant wildlife and the landmass covered by the
Western Alaska Council. This Council's geographic area is equivalent in size to the area
from San Diego to Nashville and from Omaha to San Antonio. The trees represent the forest area of South Central Alaska, home of the second largest national forest in the U.S.
(Chugach National Forest). The mountains symbolize the towering peaks of the Alaska,
Talkeetna, and Chugach mountain ranges. The tallest peak in North America—Denali (also
known as Mt. McKinley), looks down on the vastness of the Western Alaska Council. The
colored sky rising above the mountains represents the "northern lights," the beautiful aurora seen from northern Alaska.
Scout_____ Date _____ Tel_____ E-mail _____

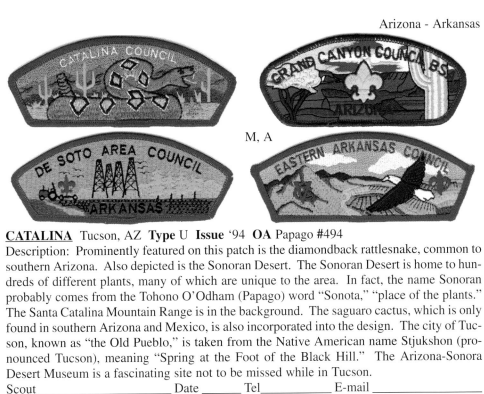

M, A

CATALINA Tucson, AZ **Type** U **Issue** '94 **OA** Papago #494
Description: Prominently featured on this patch is the diamondback rattlesnake, common to southern Arizona. Also depicted is the Sonoran Desert. The Sonoran Desert is home to hundreds of different plants, many of which are unique to the area. In fact, the name Sonoran probably comes from the Tohono O'Odham (Papago) word "Sonota," "place of the plants." The Santa Catalina Mountain Range is in the background. The saguaro cactus, which is only found in southern Arizona and Mexico, is also incorporated into the design. The city of Tucson, known as "the Old Pueblo," is taken from the Native American name Stjukshon (pronounced Tucson), meaning "Spring at the Foot of the Black Hill." The Arizona-Sonora Desert Museum is a fascinating site not to be missed while in Tucson.
Scout_____ Date _____ Tel_____ E-mail _____

GRAND CANYON Phoenix, AZ **Type** U **Issue** ____ **OA** Wipala Wiki #432
Description: This colorful CSP features the majesty of the Grand Canyon. Pictured on the left is the state tree, the paloverde. On the right is a saguaro cactus. The canyon is 217 miles long, 4 to 18 miles wide, and more than a mile deep. The plateaus and canyon walls are made up of limestone, sandstone, shale, and many other rock formations, causing the colors of the rock layers to transform with the passing daylight. This Council is headquartered in the state capital of Phoenix, Arizona. The Phoenix metro area is home to about two thirds of the state's inhabitants. The region is also home to three Native American reservations.
Scout_____ Date _____ Tel_____ E-mail _____

DE SOTO AREA El Dorado, AR **Type** U **Issue** '86 **OA** A-Booik-Paa-Gun #399
Description: This Council was named for Hernando de Soto, the Spanish explorer whose army traveled through the area in the 1530's and 1540's. The design signifies the primary economic interests of southern Arkansas. The tractor and the fertile brown soil represent the many farms of the Mississippi Delta. Also shown are typical row crops. The four oil derricks pay tribute to the petroleum industry. The four pine trees signify the forest products industries. The "four" items represent the Council's four districts. The birds in flight and the river illustrate the importance of the area's natural resources.
Scout_____ Date _____ Tel_____ E-mail _____

EASTERN ARKANSAS Jonesboro, AR **Type** U **Issue** '93 **OA** Hi'Lo Ha Chy'a-La #413
Description: This patch was designed by a committee and depicts the American bald eagle, the symbol of the ultimate rank in Scouting. It also represents the Mississippi Fly-Way. The three rivers shown from left to right are: the Black River, the L'Anguille River, and the Mississippi River. The hills on the left represent the Ozark foothills and the home of Camp Cedar Valley, the Council's Scout camp.
Scout_____ Date _____ Tel_____ E-mail _____

A

A

OUACHITA AREA Hot Springs, AR **Type** U **Issue** 3/97 **OA** Wazhazee #366
Description: This CSP pictures a beautiful sunset peeking out from behind the Ouachita Mountains. The red and blue tents, the canoeists floating on the lake, and the trees represent the tremendous outdoor program opportunities within the Council. The trees also symbolize the area's major forest products industry. The lake shown is one of six area lakes formed when the Ouachita River was dammed. This patch was designed by Mark Anderson, Scout Executive. Pike County, Arkansas, one of the six counties served by this Council, contains Crater of Diamonds State Park, the only diamond mine in the United States. Visitors may keep any diamonds found. The Council area is also home to Hot Springs National Park.
Scout_____ Date _____ Tel_____ E-mail _____

QUAPAW AREA Little Rock, AR **Type** U **Issue** ____ **OA** Quapaw #160
Description: Arkansas is a French variant of the word Quapaw, meaning "Downstream People." It was the name of the Native American tribe (Siouan people) which inhabited most of the Arkansas River Valley. The building pictured is the State Capitol of Arkansas and is patterned after the U.S. Capitol in Washington, D.C. The pine trees symbolize the many pine forests of central Arkansas and the timber industry. The river is symbolic of the Arkansas River. Flying high in the upper right are ducks. Duck hunting is an important pastime and contributes greatly to the area's economy.
Scout_____ Date _____ Tel_____ E-mail _____

WESTARK AREA Fort Smith, AR **Type** U **Issue** '93 **OA** Wachtschu Mawachpo #559
Description: The mountains and rivers pictured on this CSP make up the majority of the Council's area, which is located in the western third of Arkansas. The region contains plenty of camping and recreational space. The hog is the logo of the University of Arkansas. The Scout is looking toward the bright future developed through Scouting. In 1817, the city of Fort Smith grew up around a fort built. A new fort, established in 1838, is now a National Historic Site. In 1875, the fort became the Federal Court building. The gallows used by the famous "hanging judge" Isaac C. Parker may still be seen.
Scout_____ Date _____ Tel_____ E-mail _____

ALAMEDA Alameda, CA **Type** U **Issue** ____ **OA** Kaweah #379
Description: This Council's name, Alameda, is Spanish and translates to "Poplar Grove." The Council is located in western California in the San Francisco Bay area. The CSP stresses the Council's connection to the water. Pictured is the San Francisco-Oakland Bay Bridge —one of the longest combination bridges in the world, a sailboat, and a sea gull. Alameda Naval Air Station (closed in 1997) and a major United States Coast Guard base are located here, further identifying the area's water ties.
Scout_____ Date _____ Tel_____ E-mail _____

B, A

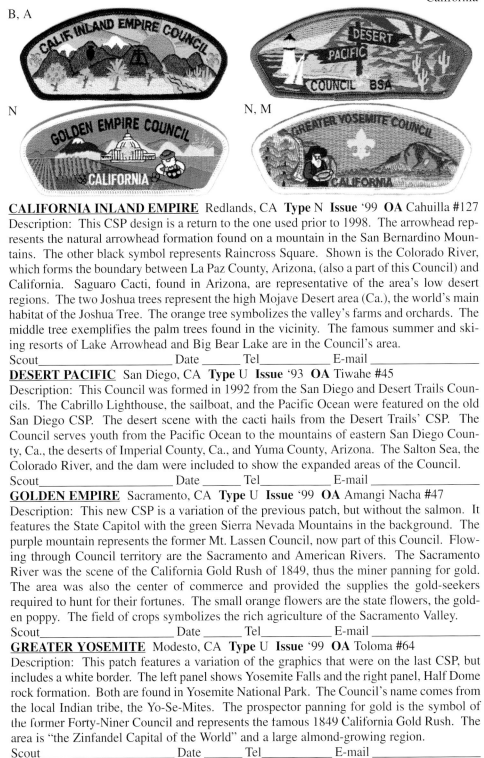

N

N, M

CALIFORNIA INLAND EMPIRE Redlands, CA **Type** N **Issue** '99 **OA** Cahuilla #127
Description: This CSP design is a return to the one used prior to 1998. The arrowhead represents the natural arrowhead formation found on a mountain in the San Bernardino Mountains. The other black symbol represents Raincross Square. Shown is the Colorado River, which forms the boundary between La Paz County, Arizona, (also a part of this Council) and California. Saguaro Cacti, found in Arizona, are representative of the area's low desert regions. The two Joshua trees represent the high Mojave Desert area (Ca.), the world's main habitat of the Joshua Tree. The orange tree symbolizes the valley's farms and orchards. The middle tree exemplifies the palm trees found in the vicinity. The famous summer and skiing resorts of Lake Arrowhead and Big Bear Lake are in the Council's area.
Scout_____ Date _____ Tel_____ E-mail _____

DESERT PACIFIC San Diego, CA **Type** U **Issue** '93 **OA** Tiwahe #45
Description: This Council was formed in 1992 from the San Diego and Desert Trails Councils. The Cabrillo Lighthouse, the sailboat, and the Pacific Ocean were featured on the old San Diego CSP. The desert scene with the cacti hails from the Desert Trails' CSP. The Council serves youth from the Pacific Ocean to the mountains of eastern San Diego County, Ca., the deserts of Imperial County, Ca., and Yuma County, Arizona. The Salton Sea, the Colorado River, and the dam were included to show the expanded areas of the Council.
Scout_____ Date _____ Tel_____ E-mail _____

GOLDEN EMPIRE Sacramento, CA **Type** U **Issue** '99 **OA** Amangi Nacha #47
Description: This new CSP is a variation of the previous patch, but without the salmon. It features the State Capitol with the green Sierra Nevada Mountains in the background. The purple mountain represents the former Mt. Lassen Council, now part of this Council. Flowing through Council territory are the Sacramento and American Rivers. The Sacramento River was the scene of the California Gold Rush of 1849, thus the miner panning for gold. The area was also the center of commerce and provided the supplies the gold-seekers required to hunt for their fortunes. The small orange flowers are the state flowers, the golden poppy. The field of crops symbolizes the rich agriculture of the Sacramento Valley.
Scout_____ Date _____ Tel_____ E-mail _____

GREATER YOSEMITE Modesto, CA **Type** U **Issue** '99 **OA** Toloma #64
Description: This patch features a variation of the graphics that were on the last CSP, but includes a white border. The left panel shows Yosemite Falls and the right panel, Half Dome rock formation. Both are found in Yosemite National Park. The Council's name comes from the local Indian tribe, the Yo-Se-Mites. The prospector panning for gold is the symbol of the former Forty-Niner Council and represents the famous 1849 California Gold Rush. The area is "the Zinfandel Capital of the World" and a large almond-growing region.
Scout_____ Date _____ Tel_____ E-mail _____

California
N

LONG BEACH AREA Long Beach, CA **Type** U **Issue** '99 **Tribe** Tahquitz
Description: This new 80th anniversary CSP was chosen via a contest. At its right is the Queen Mary, one of the world's most famous passenger liners. Behind the ship is the dome that once housed the Spruce Goose, the gigantic wooden plane built by Howard Hughs. The dome is now used as a movie sound stage. The plane represents the Long Beach Airport and the area's plane manufacturing industry. The racecar and checkered flag stand for the Long Beach Toyota Grand Prix. The three "smoke stacks" (the city's logo) are actually disguised oil derricks. They and the oil rigs on the left symbolize Signal Hill and the oil industry. The oil found at Signal Hill, located in the middle of the city, was responsible for Long Beach's origins. Note, this Council does not have an OA lodge. The Tribe of Tahquitz is an honor Scout organization separate from the National Order of the Arrow.
Scout_____ Date _____ Tel_____ E-mail _____

LOS ANGELES AREA Los Angeles, CA **Type** U **Issue** '91 **OA** Siwinis #252
Description: In this "City of Angels" Council patch, the blue represents the Pacific Ocean and the sailboat symbolizes the Port of Los Angeles. The city is located between the Pacific Ocean and the San Gabriel Mountains. The mountains can be seen behind the golden fleur-de-lis. The area is home to many forms of recreation and climate changes. Here, you can boat in the ocean and an hour later drive to the mountains and snow ski. The culturally diverse city is the second most populated one in the country. Visitors may enjoy a trip to the La Brea Tar Pits to view ice-age fossils, shop on world famous Rodeo Drive—an exclusive and expensive shopping area, or tour Beverly Hills—home to many of the rich and famous. The city's Hollywood area is well known for its movie and television industry.
Scout_____ Date _____ Tel_____ E-mail _____

LOS PADRES Santa Barbara, CA **Type** N **Issue** '93 **OA** Chumash #90
Description: This Council was formed in 1993 from the merger of Mission and Santa Lucia Area Councils. It covers the entire central coast of California and both San Luis Obispo and Santa Barbara counties. The name Los Padres is Spanish for "the Fathers," a reference to the Spanish clergy who settled there. The CSP's design was chosen via a contest and is based on a Scout's design. It incorporates the Ynez Mountains and features three hiking Scouts.
Scout_____ Date _____ Tel_____ E-mail _____

MARIN San Rafael, CA **Type** U **Issue** '88 **OA** Talako #533
Description: The word Marin is the Hispanic surname "Sailor." On this patch is the famous Golden Gate Bridge, one of the world's longest suspension bridges. It is built across the entrance (Golden Gate) to San Francisco Bay. This area was nicknamed "the Golden Gate" since it was the gateway to the "gold in them, thar' hills." The "hill" pictured is Mt. Tamalpais. The gray area represents the infamous San Francisco fog.
Scout_____ Date _____ Tel_____ E-mail _____

M

MONTEREY BAY AREA Salinas, CA **Type** U **Issue** '98 **OA** Esselen #531
Description: Featured on this patch are the tall redwood trees found in the area and at the Council's camp, Pico Blanco. The Pico Blanco Mountains, which give the camp its name, are pictured rising against the sky. The building is Mission San Carlos Borromeo Del Rio Carmelo or Carmel Mission. The golf course shown represents Pebble Beach, Cypress Point, Spy Glass Hill, and Monterey Peninsula courses. The tree is the lone cypress, a regional favorite. The blue at the CSP's bottom represents the Pacific Ocean. The brown road represents Seventeen-Mile Drive, a scenic route leading from Pacific Grove to Carmel.
Scout_____ Date _____ Tel_____ E-mail _____
MT. DIABLO SILVERADO Pleasant Hill, CA **Type** N **Issue** _____ **OA** Ut-In Sélica #58
Description: This CSP uses images from the two Councils that formed the Mt. Diablo Silverado Council. The brown bear is the California state emblem. On the right are symbols from the former Mt. Diablo Council: the 3,849-foot Mt. Diablo, the Port of Benicia, the oil tanker—symbol of the area's oil refineries, and the buildings—signifying the region's industrial parks. On the left, from Silverado Council are: Mt. Saint Helens, grapes—symbolizing the Napa Valley wine country, and a ship and water—symbols of the Bay Area, the Delta region, Mare Island, and the shipping industry. The two fleurs-de-lis signify the merger.
Scout_____ Date _____ Tel_____ E-mail _____
OLD BALDY Ontario, CA **Type** U **Issue** 9/97 **OA** Navajo #98
Description: Mt. Baldy, a part of the San Gabriel Range of southern California, is pictured in front of a magnificent rainbow colored sky. "Old Baldy" may be viewed from the 40-mile scenic road, Rim of the World Drive. Ontario, California is the site of the Los Angeles area's second international airport. Although the city is now largely residential, it was once a major agricultural center. Visitors may tour the Graber Olive House where, during the fall harvesting season, they may watch the curing, grading, and canning of olives. This CSP was designed by Scouter Suzanne Lentchner.
Scout_____ Date _____ Tel_____ E-mail _____
ORANGE COUNTY Costa Mesa, CA **Type** U **Issue** 1/96 **OA** Wiatava #13
Description: The orange, pictured on the left, represents the orange trees that once spread throughout Orange County and serves as a reminder of the area's agricultural history. The ocean and sailboats symbolize the great beaches and sailing in this area of the Pacific Ocean. Also pictured is a magnificent omega effect. The effect, possible only on a clear day, occurs when the setting sun reflects on the water at the western horizon and forms what appears to be the last letter of the Greek alphabet, omega. Orange County, blessed with many clear days, has many beautiful sunsets. The Council area is home to two very popular attractions—Disneyland and Knott's Berry Farm. This CSP was designed by Carina Reide.
Scout_____ Date _____ Tel_____ E-mail _____

PACIFIC SKYLINE Palo Alto, CA **Type** U **Issue** 1/94 **OA** Ohlone #63
Description: This Council's name was chosen because the majority of the Council is on California's west coast bordered by the Pacific Ocean and because Skyline Boulevard runs the length of the Council through its center. The CSP design was chosen via a contest in September 1993. The winning patch is bold, simple, and reflects the geographical area and majesty of this region. The city of Palo Alto (Spanish for redwood tree) was named for the ancient redwood tree that stands at the northern entrance to the city. The Council's territory is in the heart of "Silicon Valley." Palo Alto is home to Stanford University.
Scout_____ Date _____ Tel_____ E-mail _____

PIEDMONT Piedmont, CA **Type** N **Issue** _____ **OA** Hungteetsepoppi #466
Description: This Council is in an area rich in Scottish heritage. Its patch features traditional Scottish Tartan colors, the official colors of the area—orange and purple. The purple rectangle represents a field of purple heather flowers. The bridges are the Golden Gate and the Bay Bridge, which span the ocean and the bay around San Francisco. The date "1921" represents the Council's charter year.
Scout_____ Date _____ Tel_____ E-mail _____

REDWOOD EMPIRE Santa Rosa, CA **Type** N **Issue** '98 **OA** Orca #194
Description: This Council is located in the heart of Sonoma County, in northwestern California. It is a rich agricultural and wine-producing region. In fact, Sonoma is the second largest grape producer in the United States and includes part of the world famous Napa Valley wine country. The area is also known for redwood trees, farming, salmon fishing, rivers, the ocean, grapes, vineyards, and mountains, all of which are represented on the patch. Santa Rosa is home to the Robert Ripley Museum honoring native son Robert Ripley, author of "Believe It or Not." The museum is located in the Church of One Tree, so named to reflect that all the lumber used in the building came from just one redwood tree.
Scout_____ Date _____ Tel_____ E-mail _____

SAN FRANCISCO BAY AREA Oakland, CA **Type** U **Issue**___ **OA** Achewon Nimat #282
Description: This CSP pictures the San Francisco-Oakland Bay Bridge (also known as the Bay Bridge) in all its glory, against a bright orange sun. The more than eight-mile long bridge links San Francisco with the cities of East Bay. The Bay is one of the world's largest land-locked harbors. The structure on the left is the Oakland-Alameda County Coliseum Complex, which contains a stadium, indoor arena, and exhibit hall. It is here that the Oakland A's (baseball), the Raiders (football), and the Warriors (basketball) play. Jack London, the famous writer of *The Call of the Wild*, was an early resident of Oakland. A waterfront shopping and dining area, Jack London Square, was named in his honor.
Scout_____ Date _____ Tel_____ E-mail _____

SAN GABRIEL VALLEY Pasadena, CA **Type** U **Issue** '99 **OA** Ta Tanka #488
Description: This exciting new patch symbolizes the Council's past, present, and future, a recent Scout-a-rama theme. The past is represented by the southern wall of the Mission San Gabriel Arcangel, founded September 8, 1771. The mountains shown are the San Gabriel Mountains. They, along with the palm trees, indicate the Council area's present geography. The astronomically studded fleur-de-lis represents the future and the Jet Propulsion Laboratory (JPL) at the California Institute of Technology. JPL, a part of the National Aeronautics and Space Administration (NASA), has aided in the development of many spacecraft and observing instruments, such as Voyager 1 & 2 and the Hubble Space Telescope. In July 1997, they were involved in the Pathfinder and Sojourner rover's mission to Mars .
Scout_____ Date _____ Tel_____ E-mail _____

SANTA CLARA COUNTY San Jose, CA **Type** U **Issue** 4/81 **OA** Miwok #439
Description: This CSP, designed by Eagle Scout, Mark Deady, depicts the Santa Clara Valley with its agricultural base. There are more than 50 wineries here. Also depicted is the influence of the region's electronics industry. San Jose is known as the "Capital of Silicon Valley," a nickname acquired due to the area's computer-chip production and technology based industries. Surrounding the Valley are the Santa Cruz Mountains on the west and Mt. Hamilton on the east. Atop the 4,209-foot Mt. Hamilton is the Lick Observatory, home of the University of California at Santa Cruz's 120-inch telescope.
Scout_____ Date _____ Tel_____ E-mail _____

SEQUOIA Fresno, CA **Type** U **Issue** ____ **OA** Tah-Heetch #195
Description: Featured on this CSP are the Sierra Nevada Mountain Range, Yosemite Valley, and the blue waters of the Merced River. The Council is named for the region's giant sequoia trees, many of which are 200-feet high and 30-feet in diameter. The pinecones symbolize these trees. Sequoia National Park and Kings Canyon National Park are nearby. The area is a leading agricultural region specializing in grapes, figs, and cotton. Also, more turkeys are raised in this area than anywhere else in the United States.
Scout_____ Date _____ Tel_____ E-mail _____

SOUTHERN SIERRA Bakersfield, CA **Type** U **Issue** '85 **OA** Yowlumne #303
Description: The sun rising over the Sierra Nevada Mountains and a cactus are shown on this CSP. The Council includes parts of the Sierra Nevadas, the Mojave Desert, and the southern end of the San Joaquin Valley. It is home to the California Living Museum and the Tule Elk (dwarf elk) State Reserve. Bakersfield was named for Colonel Thomas Baker, whose alfalfa field was open to travelers to use to feed their horses. Bakersfield is California's country music capital and the birthplace of music star Merle Haggard.
Scout_____ Date _____ Tel_____ E-mail _____

California - Colorado

VENTURA COUNTY Camarillo, CA **Type** U **Issue** '72 **OA** Topa Topa #291
Description: The majestic bird in the foreground of the patch is the California condor, the
Council's symbol. The California condor has been considered the most endangered species
of bird in the United States. In 1988, the U.S. Fish and Wildlife Service removed the birds
from the wild and began a captive-breeding program. Some of the hatchlings born in cap-
tivity, have recently been returned to the wild. In the background, the mountains rising from
the water illustrate that the Council is located on the coast of the Pacific Ocean. The Ventura County area has an ancient Native American background dating back as far as 1600 B.C.
Scout_____ Date _____ Tel_____ E-mail _____

VERDUGO HILLS Glendale, CA **Type** U **Issue** '97 **OA** Spi-Li-Yai #249
Description: This Council's name is taken from the Verdugo Mountains, a local range. The
office is located in Glendale, Ca., at the east entrance to the San Fernando Valley. The hat
represents that Glendale was the site of the first Spanish land grant in California (Rancho
San Rafael). King Charles IV of Spain gave the grant in 1784. The shape of the state of
California is pictured in gold. The black section points to the location of the Council within the state. This residential suburb of Los Angeles depends on the film animation and technology industries for its economy. The famous Forest Lawn Memorial Park, burial site for
many past film celebrities, is located here.
Scout_____ Date _____ Tel_____ E-mail _____

WESTERN LA COUNTY Van Nuys, CA **Type** U **Issue** '89 **OA** Malibu #566
Description: This CSP features the Santa Monica Mountains and the Pacific Ocean. Emer-
ald Bay Scout Camp is located in the Pacific on Catalina Island. Pardee Seabase Scout
Camp, represented by the sailboat, is on the mainland coast at Marina Del Rey. The palm
trees pictured have come to symbolize the southern California area, although they are not
native to the region. The trees to the right of the flag decorated fleur-de-lis are members of
the Yucca genus of plants, known as the mission bell or Quixote plant (Yucca whipplei).
Scout_____ Date _____ Tel_____ E-mail _____

DENVER AREA Denver, CO **Type** U **Issue** '76? **OA** Tahosa #383
Description: The "Mile High City," as Denver is known, is the capital of Colorado. The
"C," the sun, and sky colors are from the Colorado flag. Although some units are in the
foothills, the view most of the Council sees to its west is the snow covered Rocky Mountains. The region has a large system of parks with 17 publicly owned mountain areas in a
72-mile radius, incorporating about 14,000 acres in the foothills of the Rockies. The mountains are colored purple, as represented in the song, "America the Beautiful." The trees stand
for the many forest areas in the Rockies.
Scout_____ Date _____ Tel_____ E-mail _____

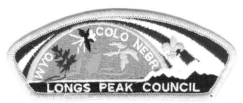

A

LONGS PEAK Greeley, CO **Type** U **Issue** '86 **OA** Kola #464
Description: This Council is comprised of areas from three states. Each state is represented within the patch by its state flower. The red flower is the Indian paintbrush of Wyoming, the blue flower is the columbine of Colorado, and the yellow flower is the goldenrod of Nebraska. The mountains pictured are the Rocky Mountains. The Council's name is derived from the tallest peak in the Council territory, Longs Peak, which towers more than 14,000-feet high at its zenith.
Scout_____ Date _____ Tel_____ E-mail _____

PIKES PEAK Colorado Springs, CO **Type** U **Issue** '83 **OA** Ha-Kin-Skay-A-Ki #387
Description: The Pikes Peak Council shoulder patch incorporates the four colors of the Colorado state flag, with the addition of green. The green trees in the foreground stress the beauty of Pikes Peak and the mountainous Front Range. The four flag colors represent Colorado's red soil, white snow-capped mountains, clear blue skies, and Pikes Peak, which is topped by the golden fleur-de-lis. These colors are symbols of the rich mountaintop experience of Scouting in the Pikes Peak Council. Pikes Peak was named after Zebulon Montgomery Pike, an American explorer, who led an expedition to this area of Colorado.
Scout_____ Date _____ Tel_____ E-mail _____

ROCKY MOUNTAIN Pueblo, CO **Type** U **Issue** ____
                    OA Tupwee (Tupwee Gudas Gov Youchiquot Soovep) #536
Description: This Council is located in Pueblo, Colorado in the eastern foothills of the Rocky Mountains. This CSP features the majestic Rockies in purple with white snow covering the high peaks. The red "C" and the yellow sun-shaped "O" symbolize the Council's Colorado location. The Scout fleur-de-lis is shown in red. Pueblo (Spanish for town) is home to the Consumer Information Center of the United States General Services Administration. The center offers many free publications on topics of interest to consumers.
Scout_____ Date _____ Tel_____ E-mail _____

WESTERN COLORADO Grand Junction, CO **Type** N **Issue** '98 **OA** Mic-O-Say #541
Description: This patch was designed by Garry Brewer and celebrates the selection of the Council's new Council Executive, Keith Alder. The eagle represents the strength of the Western Colorado Council as it soars into the 21st century. The eagle is also the OA lodge totem. The five stars represent the five districts that make up the Council. The dark-blue night sky symbolizes the clear, clean air found in Colorado. The "C" from the center of the Colorado flag signifies that the Council is within the state of Colorado. The green hills, mountains, mesas, and trees represent the hope of leaving the earth better than we found it.
Scout_____ Date _____ Tel_____ E-mail _____

Connecticut

A

A

CONNECTICUT RIVERS East Hartford, CT **Type** N **Issue** 5/95 **OA** Tschitani #10
Description: This Council, formed in 1995, is made up of the former Long Rivers and Indian Trails Councils. This patch features the mountain laurel, the state flower. The shape of the state of Connecticut, along with the state's major rivers, was the symbol found on Long Rivers' CSP. The Cardinal was the totem of the Indian Trails' Council camp.
Scout_____ Date _____ Tel_____ E-mail _____

CONNECTICUT YANKEE Norwalk, CT **Type** R **Issue** '98 **OA** Owaneco #313
Council "72" was formed from the merger of Fairfield County and Quinnipiac Councils. The Council name represents that two Scout Councils have come together and that Yankee ingenuity will guide the new Council. The water shown is Long Island Sound. The tall sailing ship represents the region's strong shipping and trade heritage. The two stars on the CSP represent truth and knowledge. The Sequassen Constellation above the ship represents one of the Council's Scout camps, Camp Sequassen. The Council's new motto "Proud of our past. Leading the future" is seen at the top of the patch. The state of Connecticut with the territories the Council serves, is also shown. One of the area's highlights is the Maritime Center at Norwalk. The Center gives visitors a glimpse of the region's maritime history and marine life through hands-on exhibits. Dan Malinak designed this CSP.
Scout_____ Date _____ Tel_____ E-mail _____

GREENWICH Greenwich, CT **Type** R **Issue** _____ **OA** Achewon Netopalis #427
Description: This CSP depicts Long Island Sound with its beautiful beaches and marinas. Also shown is the area's rich green countryside. The church is the Second Congregational Church. It is the highest point north of New York City, between N.Y.C., and Boston. It symbolizes the importance of religion in New England and Scouting. Lastly, notice the "green witch" and the Council's number, "67." Greenwich became a permanent community in 1640, when the land was purchased from local Native Americans for 25 coats.
Scout_____ Date _____ Tel_____ E-mail _____

HOUSATONIC Derby, CT **Type** R **Issue** '74 **OA** Paugassett #553
Description: Beside the Housatonic and Naugatuck Rivers lived two tribes: the Paugasetts and the Pootatucks (Algonquin). In 1614, Captain Adrian Block and Cornelius Hedrickson sailed here from Holland to establish Native American fur trading. Block led an exploration party along the wooded shores of Connecticut and discovered the Housatonic, naming it "The River of the Red Hills." This CSP is shows a Paugassett brave watching a ship. The ship, exploring the river, is about to drop anchor for the night. The brave is unaware that the sun is also about to set on his Indian nation. This area was a trading post, then a haven for settlers, and finally a home to many industries. The time, talents, and devotion of the Council's volunteers flow endlessly, like the waters of the Housatonic.
Scout_____ Date _____ Tel_____ E-mail _____

N, A

A

DEL-MAR-VA Wilmington, DE **Type** U **Issue** _____ **OA** Nentego #20
Description: This Council's name denotes the areas it serves: Delaware, Maryland, and Virginia. This area is known as the Del-Mar-Va Peninsula. The CSP pictures a tractor, symbolizing the importance of farming in the area. Also pictured are the skyscrapers of Wilmington, the Chesapeake Bay Bridge, and a sailboat that reminds us of the region's great boating activities. Wilmington is the largest city in Delaware and is noted for its chemical industry. It is here, since 1802, that E.I. du Pont de Nemours and Company is based. Places to visit in the city include the Winterthur Museum and Longwood Gardens.
Scout_____ Date _____ Tel_____ E-mail _____

CENTRAL FLORIDA Orlando, FL **Type** U **Issue** '99 **OA** Tipisa #326
Description: This new CSP, designed by John Fisher, is a take-off on an older design. The scene moves from left to right just as the Council extends from the the coast to the inlands. A space shuttle is seen heading toward the sky. It represents the Kennedy Space Center and the area's aerospace industry. The fleur-de-lis is engulfed in the crescent moon, reminder of the Apollo missions. The moon forms a "C" for central Florida. The orange trees symbolize the region's renown as one of the nation's most important citrus growing centers. The Council is home to one of the United States' most popular vacation attractions, Walt Disney World. Sea World and Universal Studios Florida Theme Park are also in the Council's area.
Scout_____ Date _____ Tel_____ E-mail _____

GULF COAST Pensacola, FL **Type** U **Issue** _____ **OA** Yustaga #385
Description: This Council, covering areas in Alabama and Florida, pays homage to its Spanish heritage with the Spanish shield found on the left side. The Council's camp is known as Spanish Trail Scout Reservation. Fort Pickins is seen on the right. Fort Pickins, built from 1829 to 1834, was one of the forts used to protect Pensacola Harbor during the Civil War. The word "Pensacola" is Native American for " Long-haired People." The six pine trees stand for the six districts that form this Council. A major portion of the area's economy is derived from the Pensacola Naval Air Station and other U.S. Navy installations.
Scout_____ Date _____ Tel_____ E-mail _____

GULF RIDGE Tampa, FL **Type** U **Issue** _____ **OA** Seminole #85
Description: The bird depicted is a white ibis, which is native to Florida. The ibis was also adopted as the Council's OA Lodge totem. The two palm trees represent the many palms found throughout Florida. A blue background was chosen to symbolize the clear blue Gulf of Mexico waters. The red, in front of the green land, represents the sun's reflection on the Gulf. Of course, the circular yellow sun stands for Florida, also known as "the Sunshine State." "Tampa" is Calusa Native American and means "Lightning."
Scout_____ Date _____ Tel_____ E-mail _____

Florida

M, A

GULF STREAM West Palm Beach, FL **Type** U **Issue** _____ **OA** Aal-Pa-Tah #237
Description: Prominently featured on this CSP is the alligator. This marine reptile found lounging on a log plays an important role in this Council and is seen throughout the region. The brilliant sunset shines over the Council's riverside camp, Aal-Pa-Tah, which means "alligator" in the Seminole language. In addition, the alligator is the Council's mascot. The Seminole Indians have a proud history in the area and are famous for their ability to handle the alligator. On the patch's left, a Seminole is shown facing this frightening animal.
Scout_____ Date _____ Tel_____ E-mail _____

NORTH FLORIDA Jacksonville, FL **Type** U **Issue** _____ **OA** Echockotee #200
Description: This CSP features the flags of the governments that once ruled Florida. The flags are, from left to right: the Spanish flag that Christopher Columbus brought to the New World, the Confederate flag, the Stars and Stripes of the U.S., the blue-and-yellow flag brought by the French explorers, and the British flag brought by the Pilgrims. Some of the cities the Council serves are: St. Augustine—the oldest permanent European settlement in the U.S. (1565) and the 1513 landing site of Spanish explorer Juan Ponce de León, who was searching for the Fountain of Youth, Gainsville—home to the University of Florida, and Ocala—location of the beautiful Ocala National Forest.
Scout_____ Date _____ Tel_____ E-mail _____

SOUTH FLORIDA Miami Lakes, FL **Type** U **Issue** _____ **OA** O-Shot-Caw #265
Description: This patch depicts the south Florida sunshine with the golden sky and the bright orange sun reflecting on the Caribbean-blue Atlantic Ocean. Palm trees, found throughout Florida, are pictured in the lower left. The pink flamingo, a popular bird found in the sub-tropical climate of Florida, is also shown. The region is home to the largest sub-tropical wilderness in the United States, Everglades National Park. The Miami area is a large international community. It is also experiencing a renaissance as a popular tourist destination. The beautiful art-deco buildings of the region are being restored and are once again in high demand.
Scout_____ Date _____ Tel_____ E-mail _____

SOUTHWEST FLORIDA Fort Myers, FL **Type** N **Issue** '92 **OA** Osceola #564
Description: This patch, designed by David Mott, features the Florida panther, the state animal. The panther is set against a pinewood background, reminiscent of Camp Miles, a Council Scout camp. The Council incorporates all of southwest Florida from Manatee to Collier County. The winter homes of Henry Ford and Thomas Alva Edison are located in Council territory. The homes are open for public viewing.
Scout_____ Date _____ Tel_____ E-mail _____

M

M

SUWANNEE RIVER AREA Tallahassee, FL **Type** U **Issue**____ **OA** Semialachee #239
Description: This patch shows replicas of the Florida and Georgia flags, and represents the
areas served by this Council. The Council gets its name from the Suwannee River (made
famous in the popular song) that borders the Council's territory on the east. The Council is
headquartered in Tallahassee, the state capital of Florida. The city is home to Florida State
University, with its championship winning Seminole football team and Florida A&M University, where the Black Archives Research Center and Museum is located.
Scout_____ Date _____ Tel_____ E-mail _____

WEST CENTRAL FLORIDA Seminole, FL **Type** U **Issue** '70's **OA** Timuquan #340
Description: This Council covers the Tampa Bay Area, which includes St. Petersburg, and
Clearwater. The patch features the state seal and flag of Florida. These symbols have been
used by special permission from the Governor and State Cabinet. Although the Council is
geographically small, only 60 miles long and 10 miles wide, it is within one of the most
densely populated areas in Florida. There are 10,000 boys and 3,000 adults in this Council's Scouting program. St Petersburg, Tampa's sister city, is a major tourist destination. It
is home to the Salvador Dali Museum, which houses North America's largest collection of
the surrealist artist's works. Clearwater is noted for its beautiful sandy beaches.
Scout_____ Date _____ Tel_____ E-mail _____

ALAPAHA AREA Valdosta, GA **Type** U **Issue** '64 **OA** Alapaha #545
Description: The name of this Council comes from the Alapaha River ("Clear Water" in
Native American). Mr. Ralph Smith was the designer of this patch. Mr. Smith is retired
from the military and is also an accomplished archer. He has taught many Scouts his archery
talent. On the patch, the red within the blue section of the map is the Alapaha Area Council territory. The Council incorporates 12 counties. Valdosta is also known as the "Gateway
to Florida" because of its proximity to the much-traveled Interstate 75. The city's name is
taken from the name of the governor's home "Val de Aosta" (Spanish) or "Vale of Beauty."
Scout_____ Date _____ Tel_____ E-mail _____

ATLANTA AREA Atlanta, GA **Type** U **Issue** ____ **OA** Egwa Tawa Dee #129
Description: This Council is located in the capital city of Atlanta, Georgia. Atlanta, an international city, is a hub of industry, finance, and commerce. It mixes today's modern-city look
with "Old South" ambiance. Atlanta played host to the 1996 Olympics. This CSP was
designed by Louis (Rick) Rickman. The abstract symbol depicts a phoenix rising out of
flames, just as Atlanta rose from the ashes and devastation of the Civil War to its current
position of prominence in southern culture and business. Things to visit while in Atlanta
include: The World of Coca-Cola Museum, Atlanta Cyclorama, the CNN Studio, The Carter
Center, The Martin Luther King, Jr. Center and the Six Flags Over Atlanta Theme Park.
Scout_____ Date _____ Tel_____ E-mail _____

Georgia

A

M

CENTRAL GEORGIA Macon, GA **Type** U **Issue** _____ **OA** Echeconnee #358
Description: Pictured on this patch is historic Fort Hawkin, built in 1806 by Thomas Jefferson. A replica of the fort may be visited in Macon, Georgia. Fort Hawkin, a Macon landmark, is named after Benjamin Hawkin, the famous statesman, Revolutionary War veteran, and Indian agent. The city of Macon is reputed to be the only city in the southeast that owes its start to a frontier fort.
Scout_____ Date _____ Tel_____ E-mail _____

CHATTAHOOCHEE Columbus, GA **Type** U **Issue** '82 **OA** Chattahoochee #204
Description: The Chattahoochee River, which runs through 10 of the 15 counties within this Council, gives the Council its name. Although this Council is based in western Georgia, its area extends in to Alabama. Columbus, a port city on the Chattahoochee River, is directly across from Phenix City, Alabama. A bridge connects the two states. The leaf and acorns found on the patch represent the Georgia state tree, the live oak. The Native American headdress and peace pipe symbolize the Native American tribes that inhabited the Council's area. Both the Creek and Yuchi peoples were found in this area.
Scout_____ Date _____ Tel_____ E-mail _____

COASTAL EMPIRE Savannah, GA **Type** U **Issue** '98 **OA** Tomo Chi-Chi #119
Description: The bird depicted on the left of this patch is the blue heron, symbol of the Council's Camp Blue Heron. The Native American is Tomo Chi Chi, chief of the Creek Indians. The Creeks were native to Savannah. Tomo Chi Chi is also the Council's lodge name. The lighthouse signifies the Tybee Island Lighthouse, which is an area icon. Home for this Council is picturesque Savannah, a perfect example of an historic "Old South" city. The city is located in southeastern Georgia on the Savannah River. Savannah is also an important city for the Girl Scouts. It was here that Juliette Gordon Low, the founder of Girl Scouts of America, was born. Her home may be visited by the public.
Scout_____ Date _____ Tel_____ E-mail _____

FLINT RIVER Griffin, GA **Type** U **Issue** '79 **OA** Ini-to #324
Description: This Council was named after the Flint River that runs through its area. The thunderbird on this patch was taken from the OA lodge totem. The Council's Camp Thunder is represented by the lightning bolt over the right shoulder of the thunderbird. Each multi-colored sunray has the name of one of the eight counties that make up the five districts of the Council. "Georgia" sits in the sun that shines over the state. John Henry "Doc" Holliday, the famous American dentist, gunfighter, and gambler, was born in Griffin, Georgia (1852-1887). Also born within the Council's territory, in Macon, Georgia, was poet Sidney Lanier (1842-1881).
Scout_____ Date _____ Tel_____ E-mail _____

M

GEORGIA-CAROLINA Augusta, GA **Type** U **Issue** 1/93 **OA** Bob White #87
Description: The river pictured is the Savannah River, which runs through the Council's territory. This Council is on a fall line with lowlands and foothills. The crossed flags symbolize the South Carolina and Georgia counties served by the Council. The sun and rays are a symbol of a new era of growth and excitement for Scouting in the Central Savannah River area. The Augusta region is a large resort and golfing center. Each year the Masters golf tournament is held at the Augusta National Golf Course. The city is also proud to be the boyhood home of President Woodrow Wilson.
Scout_____ Date _____ Tel_____ E-mail _____
NORTHEAST GEORGIA Pendergrass, GA **Type** U **Issue** '79 **OA** Mowogo #243
Description: This CSP represents gold miners, prevalent in the rolling piedmont region of northeast Georgia during the 18th and 19th centuries. The log cabin pictured was constructed in 1899 and still stands at the Council's Scout camp, Camp Rainey Mountain in Clayton, Georgia. Areas of special interest within the Council's territory include the University of Georgia, Tallulah Gorge, Lake Lanier, and the southern end of the Appalachian National Scenic Trail at Springer Mountain.
Scout_____ Date _____ Tel_____ E-mail _____
NORTHWEST GEORGIA Rome, GA **Type** U **Issue** '90 **OA** Waguli #318
Description: This patch depicts a great deal of the area's history. On the left, a Native American scene symbolizes the capital of the Cherokee tribe, which is located in this Council's service area. The Chieftains Museum, once the 18th century home of Cherokee Treaty Party leader, Major Ridge, is in this Council. On the right, is a scene of Camp Sidney Dew Cabin, the logo of the Council's camp. The background colors are representative of the beautiful rolling mountains of northwest Georgia, the sunsets, and the clear starry nights often enjoyed in this region. Although the city of Rome, Georgia, is built on seven hills, just as Rome, Italy is, it did not get its name from the Italian city. The three men who drew the plans for the Georgia city literally picked the name out of a hat.
Scout_____ Date _____ Tel_____ E-mail _____
OKEFENOKEE AREA Waycross, GA **Type** U **Issue** ____ **OA** Pilthlako #229
Description: This Council was one of the last to change from the traditional red and white lettered shoulder patch to the colorful and individual CSP style now used. The Council's name "Okefenokee" means "Land of Trembling Earth" and is derived from the Seminole Native Americans who lived in the area. Pictured is the Okefenokee Swamp, most of which is part of the Okefenokee National Wildlife Refuge. On the patch, the two different birds found in the swamp are the egret and the eider (coastal duck). The white sands represent the coastal region and the cypress trees are indicative of the ones found throughout the swamp.
Scout_____ Date _____ Tel_____ E-mail _____

A

SOUTHWEST GEORGIA Albany, GA **Type** U **Issue** _____ **OA** Immokalee #353
Description: On this CSP are seventeen sunrays and pine trees, which stand for the seventeen counties that comprise this Council. The patch honors the Creek Native Americans by featuring an Indian brave at the water's edge, canoes, and tepees. The owl represents the Council's OA Lodge, Immokalee, which means "owl" in Native American. Major crops farmed in Albany, Georgia, include pecans, peanuts, corn, and cotton. An annual pecan festival is held to celebrate the crop's importance to the area's economy.
Scout_____ Date _____ Tel_____ E-mail _____

ALOHA Honolulu, HI **Type** U **Issue** '75 **OA** Ná Mokupuni O Lawelawe #567
Description: The Council's name "Aloha" means "hello," "goodbye," and "love" in Hawaiian. The CSP represents: the State of Hawaii, Commonwealth of Northern Marianas, Republic of the Marshall Islands, Republic of Palau, Federated States of Micronesia, American Samoa, Guam, and Kwajalein. The central design represents the shape of the world, symbolizing internationalism. Also pictured is the International Dateline located within the 3,000-mile span of the Council's territory. The lotus blossom shape is a symbol of the three parts of the Scout Oath and this Council's proximity and ethnic connection to the Orient. The pyramid shaped base symbolizes the strength of trained leadership as the foundation of the Council's success. The coconut palm trees are suggestive of a Polynesian landscape.
Scout_____ Date _____ Tel_____ E-mail _____

MAUI COUNTY Wailuku, HI **Type** R **Issue** _____ **OA** Maluhia #554
Description: The three islands that comprise Maui County Council are pictured on this patch, Maui, Molokai, and Lanai. The whale represents the many whales that can be found wintering in the waters surrounding Maui. It also reminds us that the harbor town of Lahaina was once known as the "Whaling Capital of the Pacific." Maui, "the Valley Island," is the second largest of the Hawaiian islands. The dormant volcano, Haleakala, is located on this island. The islands are popular tourist, scuba diving, and snorkeling spots.
Scout_____ Date _____ Tel_____ E-mail _____

ORE-IDA Boise, ID **Type** U **Issue** '97 **OA** Tukarica #266
Description: This Council services areas in Oregon and Idaho, hence its name. Shown is Payette Lake in McCull, Idaho. The Council's Camp Morrison's waterfront is located on the lake. The wagon wheel and pickaxe, the Council's logo since it was founded in 1968, symbolize the Lewis and Clark Expedition and the "Oregon Trail" that runs through much of the Council. The CSP features mountains and pine trees that are abundantly found in the region. Boise, which means "wooded" in French, is nicknamed "the City of Trees." It is also known as the "Banana Belt" by locals, due to its mild winters. The National Interagency Fire Center, which coordinates wildfire fighting in the U. S., is located in Boise, Idaho.
Scout_____ Date _____ Tel_____ E-mail _____

N  N

N N

GRAND TETON Idaho Falls, ID **Type** R **Issue** '99 **OA** Shunkah Mahneetu #407
Description: This Council was named for the majestic Teton Mountains. It is made up of
the former Teton Peaks and Tendoy Area Councils. The Council has expressed itself with a
set of beautifully designed patches representing the four seasons. The different CSPs reflect
the colors, tasks, and landscapes of the spring, summer, fall, and winter months. Although
all four scenes take place at the same location, each is completely unique. Pictured on all
of the patches are a part of the Rocky Mountains—the magnificent Teton Mountains, featuring Grand Teton in the middle. Grand Teton is the highest peak in the range and tops out
at 13,771-feet. It is located in Grand Teton National Park, just south of Yellowstone National Park. The area was once a great hunting and fishing ground for the region's Native American population. "Spring" is represented in yellow and purple tones. A Native American
sits serenely under a single tree smoking his peacepipe and looking out over the landscape.
"Summer" features the bright blue skies and lush green lands of the season. The Native
American stands proudly holding a bird. Four trees bloom beside him. "Fall" transforms
the scene once again with its warm browns and oranges, colors of the falling leaves. A fire
is being kept aglow by the Native American. Lastly, "winter" comes upon the region and
brings the bitter cold and blankets the land in pure white snow. Now, the Native American
sits perched high atop his horse, arms outstretched, taking in the beauty and awe of his sur-
roundings.

Scout_____ Date _____ Tel_____ E-mail _____

Scout_____ Date _____ Tel_____ E-mail _____

Scout_____ Date _____ Tel_____ E-mail _____

Scout_____ Date _____ Tel_____ E-mail _____

V, A

SNAKE RIVER Twin Falls, ID **Type** R **Issue** ____ **OA** Ma I Shu #363
Description: This Council is located in southern Idaho. The great gorge of the Snake River is situated nearby. Fittingly, this patch prominently features a snake rising from the Snake River. The Snake is known for its length and many rapids, twists, and turns. Whitewater rapid fans often travel to the Snake River to enjoy its challenges.
Scout_____ Date _____ Tel_____ E-mail _____

ABRAHAM LINCOLN Springfield, IL **Type** N **Issue** ____ **OA** Illinek #132
Description: This Council is headquartered in the Illinois state capital of Springfield. The Council's CSP illustrates Lincoln's life in Central Illinois. Abraham Lincoln practiced law (1837-1861) and served as a state legislator (1834-1840) in Springfield. The log cabin represents his youth and young adulthood. He lived here when elected to the presidency. Some of the area's attractions are the Lincoln Home National Historic Site, the Abraham Lincoln Memorial Garden, and the Lincoln Tomb State Historic Site—burial place of Lincoln, his wife, and three of their sons. The three icons—the Log Cabin & Rail-splitter, Honest Abe, and the Lincoln Home— represent the three districts that form this Council.
Scout_____ Date _____ Tel_____ E-mail _____

BLACKHAWK AREA Rockford, IL **Type** N **Issue** '99 **OA** Wulapeju #140
Description: This CSP is a variation of the prior patch, but features black lettering. The Council was named for the famous Native American, Chief Black Hawk. His image is found on this patch. Black Hawk or Ma-ka-tai-me-she-kia-kiak, a member of the Sauk tribe (Algonquin), tried to retain the Rock River area for his tribe's homeland. After a series of conflicts known as the Black Hawk War, he and the few Native Americans who survived were forced westward. The body of water depicted is the Rock River that runs through the length of the Council. The mountains, known as the Mississippi Bluffs, are in the background.
Scout_____ Date _____ Tel_____ E-mail _____

CHICAGO AREA Chicago, IL **Type** U **Issue** '80 **OA** Owasippe #7
Description: The Chicago skyline is the prominent feature on this patch. Some of the notable buildings shown include the Wrigley Building, the Monadnock, the Federal Center Plaza, the First National Bank Building—the tallest bank in the world, Marina City, and the world's tallest building—the 110-story Sears Tower. The Chicago Council is located on Lake Michigan within "the Windy City." Although famous for the gusty winds from the lake, the city's nickname actually came from Chicago's reputation as a city of boisterous politicians. A sailboat is featured cruising on Lake Michigan, representing the revival of the city's riverfront area and Navy Pier. The sun in the background symbolizes the beautiful sunsets seen on the lake and the sun rising on Scouting throughout the region.
Scout_____ Date _____ Tel_____ E-mail _____

N

DES PLAINES VALLEY La Grange, IL **Type** R **Issue** _____ **OA** Pachsegink #246
Description: Illinois' greenery, the deep blue Des Plaines River's waters, and a golden sky with glowing rays emanating from the Scout fleur-de-lis are featured on this CSP. The Council is located in a southwestern suburb of Chicago. The Council is home to the world famous Brookfield Zoo. Also located in Council territory is the Chicago Portage National Historic Site. This site, in suburban Lyons, is the approximate place where early voyagers traveled between the Great Lakes and the Mississippi River by light watercraft.
Scout_____ Date _____ Tel_____ E-mail _____

LINCOLN TRAILS Decatur, IL **Type** U **Issue** '95 **OA** Woapink #167
Description: In 1830, Abraham Lincoln moved with his family to Decatur, Illinois. There, he lived in a log cabin along the Sanamon River. Lincoln gave his first political speech in Decatur in what is now known as Lincoln Square. He later moved to New Salem, Illinois, and then to Springfield, Illinois, hence the Council's name, "Lincoln Trails." On this CSP the red, white, and blue of the United States' flag are used as the background for three important Council icons. The red section pictures Lincoln, the white features the Scout emblem, and the state, and star in the blue depicts the Council's central Illinois location.
Scout_____ Date _____ Tel_____ E-mail _____

MISSISSIPPI VALLEY Quincy, IL **Type** U **Issue** _____ **OA** Ka-Ti Missi Sipi #37
Description: This Council is comprised of areas from three of the states that border the Mississippi River: Illinois, Iowa, and Missouri. The CSP features the bluffs along the Mississippi River and a combination of scenery viewed from the Council's two Scout camps, Camp Saukenauk and Camp Eastman. Camp Eastman is the country's only Scout camp located on the Mississippi River. The bald eagle perched upon the oak tree represents the area's allure as a winter roost for eagles. The eagle is also the Council's logo.
Scout_____ Date _____ Tel_____ E-mail _____

NORTHEAST ILLINOIS Highland Park, IL **Type** U **Issue** '99 **OA** Ma-Ka-Ja-Wan #40
Description: This new CSP was a committee decision. It features the compass rose superimposed by the gold Scouting fleur-de-lis. Gold was chosen to emphasize the Scouting Way. The gold star on the northeast point of the compass represents the Council. The compass also serves as a sun rising over Lake Michigan, which is the Council's eastern border. Seventy percent of the Council is located in Lake County, Illinois, while the rest is in Northeast Cook County, Illinois. The canoe and hiking Scouts symbolize the Council's strong outdoor program. The pine trees represent Camp Ma Ka Ja Wan in northern Wisconsin. Visitors to Highland Park may view three homes designed by renowned architect Frank Lloyd Wright and visit Ravinia Park, summer home of the Chicago Symphony Orchestra.
Scout_____ Date _____ Tel_____ E-mail _____

Illinois

NORTHWEST SUBURBAN Mount Prospect, IL **Type** N **Issue** '85 **OA** Lakota #175
Description: A contest was held to develop a fully embroidered patch to replace the Council's older red patch with white borders. The new CSP was designed by a Scout and features a camping scene silhouetted against a rising sun. It symbolizes an unlimited vision for the future. The Council's fires are represented by a rising smoke trail. In 1955, Ray Kroc built the first McDonald's fast food franchise restaurant in Des Plaines, Illinois, within the Council's territory. The McDonald's Museum has been erected on the original site.
Scout_____ Date _____ Tel_____ E-mail _____

OKAW VALLEY Belleville, IL **Type** N **Issue** 10/94 **OA** Taleka #81
Description: This Council's name represents the two Councils that united to form a new Council in 1965. "Okaw" is the Native American name for the Kaskaskia River and was used to represent the Kaskaskia Council. The "Valley" was used to symbolize the Mississippi Valley Council. The patch depicts the famous "Popeye" cartoon character. The creator of Popeye, E.C. Seger, grew up in Chester, Illinois, which is now called the "Home of Popeye." The Council proudly considers itself the "Home Council of Popeye." The rainbow in the background represents the six districts that comprise the Council.
Scout_____ Date _____ Tel_____ E-mail _____

PRAIRIELANDS Champaign, IL **Type** N **Issue** 4/92 **OA** Illini #55
Description: The current CSP design was the work of an Eagle Scout. He entered his design into a Council-wide contest held after the consolidation of the Arrowhead and Piankeshaw Councils into Prairielands in early 1992. The design encompasses scenes of both a rural prairie, as symbolized by the farm and tractor, and the Council area's larger communities, represented by the city buildings. Prairielands' nine county service area is one of the world's largest producers of corn and soybeans.
Scout_____ Date _____ Tel_____ E-mail _____

RAINBOW Morris, IL **Type** R **Issue** ____ **OA** Waupecan #197
Description: This Council was named Rainbow because in 1925, during a search for a new name, a group of Scouts saw a rainbow while camping at the Council camp. The canoe pictured on the patch has two people in it. On the right is Louis Joliet, and on the left is Père Jacques Marquette. Louis Joliet was a French-Canadian explorer who charted the Mississippi River. Père Marquette was an explorer and French missionary who accompanied Joliet. They were the first Europeans to travel on the Mississippi River. After their voyage, Marquette remained in Illinois to aid the Native Americans. The green represents Illinois, and the star marks the Council's location.
Scout_____ Date _____ Tel_____ E-mail _____

V

THREE FIRES St. Charles, IL **Type** N **Issue** ____ **OA** Lowaneu Allanque #41
Description: The Potowatami Indians were one of the tribes living in the Council area during the 1700's and early 1800's. Their most famous chiefs were Shabonna and Waubonsee. The Potawatamis belonged to the Algonquian language group of the eastern forest tribes. They were closely allied with the Chippewas and Ottawas. From early times, the three tribes formed a federation known as "The Three Fires." They were the last to cede their land to the U.S. government and leave Illinois. The symbols chosen were in honor of this tribal alliance and the unity of the two Councils that merged to form the Three Fires Council. The Council name and patch symbol were created by Matt Krause from Pack 140.
Scout_____ Date _____ Tel_____ E-mail _____

TRAILS WEST Wood River, IL **Type** N **Issue** '99 **OA** Kishkakon #32
Description: This patch is only a slight variation of the Council's last patch. On the left is the piasa bird, symbol of the old Piasa Bird Council. In the center are Lewis and Clark. They explored the Wood River and mapped out the Louisiana Purchase Territory. On the right is Cahokia Mound, representing the old Cahokia Mound Council. The name "Trails West" commemorates the olden days, when people journeying west passed through the area.
Scout_____ Date _____ Tel_____ E-mail _____

W.D. BOYCE Peoria, IL **Type** U **Issue** ____ **OA** Wenasa Quenhotan #23
Description: The illustration on this patch tells the story of how the Boy Scouts of America started. W.D. Boyce, an American businessman, lost in a London fog, stopped under a street lamp to find his way. An English Scout asked if he could assist him to his destination and then, refusing a tip from Mr. Boyce, stated that he was a Scout and could not accept money for doing a "Good Turn." Mr. Boyce was very impressed by this gesture and went on to bring Scouting from England to the United States. William Dixon Boyce lived and is buried in Ottawa, Illinois, a small town in this Council. The OA lodge name translates to "Home of the Founder," which is also the Council's motto.
Scout_____ Date _____ Tel_____ E-mail _____

ANTHONY WAYNE AREA Fort Wayne, IN **Type** R **Issue** ____ **OA** Kiskakon #75
Description: This Council, located in Fort Wayne in Northeast Indiana, gets its name from General "Mad" Anthony Wayne. Wayne is featured on this CSP riding in front of a stockade fort. Anthony Wayne was an American officer during and after the American Revolution. This fort represents the area's early establishment by the colonists. Fort Wayne is at a junction of three rivers: St. Mary's, St. Joseph's, and the Maumee. John Chapman, an American pioneer, commonly known as Johnny Appleseed, is buried here. The Council's camp, Chief Little Turtle, is a favorite with the area's Scouts.
Scout_____ Date _____ Tel_____ E-mail _____

Indiana

M N

M

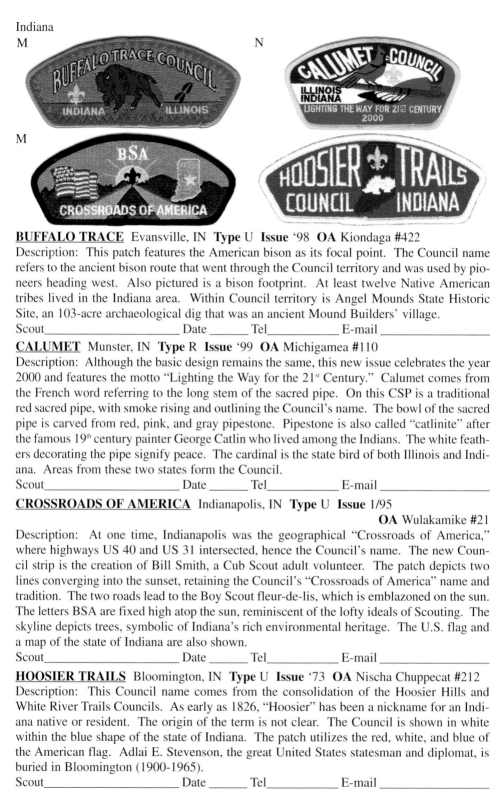

BUFFALO TRACE Evansville, IN **Type** U **Issue** '98 **OA** Kiondaga #422
Description: This patch features the American bison as its focal point. The Council name
refers to the ancient bison route that went through the Council territory and was used by pioneers heading west. Also pictured is a bison footprint. At least twelve Native American
tribes lived in the Indiana area. Within Council territory is Angel Mounds State Historic
Site, an 103-acre archaeological dig that was an ancient Mound Builders' village.
Scout_____ Date _____ Tel_____ E-mail _____

CALUMET Munster, IN **Type** R **Issue** '99 **OA** Michigamea #110
Description: Although the basic design remains the same, this new issue celebrates the year
2000 and features the motto "Lighting the Way for the 21st Century." Calumet comes from
the French word referring to the long stem of the sacred pipe. On this CSP is a traditional
red sacred pipe, with smoke rising and outlining the Council's name. The bowl of the sacred
pipe is carved from red, pink, and gray pipestone. Pipestone is also called "catlinite" after
the famous 19th century painter George Catlin who lived among the Indians. The white feathers decorating the pipe signify peace. The cardinal is the state bird of both Illinois and Indiana. Areas from these two states form the Council.
Scout_____ Date _____ Tel_____ E-mail _____

CROSSROADS OF AMERICA Indianapolis, IN **Type** U **Issue** 1/95

OA Wulakamike #21
Description: At one time, Indianapolis was the geographical "Crossroads of America,"
where highways US 40 and US 31 intersected, hence the Council's name. The new Council strip is the creation of Bill Smith, a Cub Scout adult volunteer. The patch depicts two
lines converging into the sunset, retaining the Council's "Crossroads of America" name and
tradition. The two roads lead to the Boy Scout fleur-de-lis, which is emblazoned on the sun.
The letters BSA are fixed high atop the sun, reminiscent of the lofty ideals of Scouting. The
skyline depicts trees, symbolic of Indiana's rich environmental heritage. The U.S. flag and
a map of the state of Indiana are also shown.
Scout_____ Date _____ Tel_____ E-mail _____

HOOSIER TRAILS Bloomington, IN **Type** U **Issue** '73 **OA** Nischa Chuppecat #212
Description: This Council name comes from the consolidation of the Hoosier Hills and
White River Trails Councils. As early as 1826, "Hoosier" has been a nickname for an Indiana native or resident. The origin of the term is not clear. The Council is shown in white
within the blue shape of the state of Indiana. The patch utilizes the red, white, and blue of
the American flag. Adlai E. Stevenson, the great United States statesman and diplomat, is
buried in Bloomington (1900-1965).
Scout_____ Date _____ Tel_____ E-mail _____

LA SALLE South Bend, IN **Type** U **Issue** 12/90 **OA** Sakima #573
Description: This Council, which has merged several times, has been known as the Tri Valley, Northern Indiana, and La Salle Councils. This CSP is a variation of their last CSP—Northern Indiana. In 1990, they included a part of Michigan, requiring a name change. Along with the new name, they added a cardinal and the state of Michigan to the patch. The state birds of Michigan (robin) and Indiana (cardinal) are both shown sitting on a tulip branch (the Indiana state tree). The Scout fleur-de-lis denotes the Council's location on the borders of Indiana and Michigan. The Council is named after René-Robert Cavelier Sieur de La Salle (1643-1687), the French explorer who explored much of the Council's area.
Scout_____ Date _____ Tel_____ E-mail _____

SAGAMORE Kokomo, IN **Type** U **Issue** '73 **OA** Takachsin #173
Description: The word "Sagamore" means "Chief of Chiefs" (or leader), a very fitting name for a Boy Scout Council. This CSP depicts "The Prophet," Tenskwatawa (Shawnee), brother of the great Chief Tecumseh. Tenskwatawa was a religious visionary who preached against adopting the "White Man's" ways, especially the consumption of alcohol. The Prophet is shown here wearing long hair and a feathered headdress. A peace pipe and war club are also pictured. Tecumseh and his brother's dream of forming an alliance with other Native American tribes to retain their land was crushed by William Henry Harrison at the Battle of Tippecanoe (1811). The red fleurs-de-lis are symbols of peace and of Boy Scouting everywhere. The Council is home to the birthplace of legendary actor James Dean.
Scout_____ Date _____ Tel_____ E-mail _____

WABASH VALLEY Terre Haute, IN **Type** U **Issue** ____ **OA** Kickapoo #128
Description: The moon over the Wabash River is a symbol not exclusive to either Illinois or Indiana, the states that have areas serviced by this Council. The Wabash River runs through Terre Haute, In., and forms the southwestern boundary line between the two states. The smoking campfire in the right forefront symbolizes the Council's camping program.
Scout_____ Date _____ Tel_____ E-mail _____

HAWKEYE AREA Cedar Rapids, IA **Type** U **Issue** ___ **OA** Cho-Gun-Mun-A-Nock #467
Description: This Council's name comes from the Iowa nickname, "the Hawkeye State." The name honors Chief Black Hawk, a leader of the Sauk tribe, whose people were relocated to the Cedar Rapids, Iowa area. The CSP mimics the state flag. The region is a large food processing area especially known for its breakfast cereals and is home to the Quaker Oats Company. The Amana Colonies are an area highlight. These villages were built in the mid 1850's by German immigrants and served as religious havens. Visitors are transported back in time and can see working furniture factories, wool mills, bakeries, and wineries.
Scout_____ Date _____ Tel_____ E-mail _____

Iowa

ILLOWA Davenport, IA **Type** U **Issue** _____ **OA** Konepaka Ketiwa #38
Description: This Council's name reflects the two states that it serves, Illinois and Iowa.
The American bald eagle, symbol of both America and Boy Scouting, is pictured soaring
past the sun. The Native American is Chief Black Hawk, of the Sauk (yellow earth people)
tribe. The Chief is shown holding his totem, a symbol or emblem of his family. A series of
wars, known as the Black Hawk Wars, began when the Chief disputed an agreement in which
tribal lands were sold to the U.S. government. Black Hawk claimed that tribal members
were given liquor prior to the signing of the agreement. An ambassador of peace was sent
by Black Hawk, but he was shot by the white settlers. Black Hawk and his people lost the
war (1832), and they settled on a reservation in Fort Des Moines, Iowa. Within the Council's territory is Credit Island, the 1814 site of a British victory that occurred during the War
of 1812. Credit Island is now a park.
Scout_____ Date _____ Tel_____ E-mail _____

MID-IOWA Des Moines, IA **Type** R **Issue** 12/93 **OA** Mitigwa #450
Description: This CSP was chosen as the new regular issue patch from the series of six
patches that made up the "Images of Iowa." The patch features an example of a covered
bridge, an important part of Iowa's history. Madison County boasts six covered bridges,
most still in use. This bridge is the Roseman Bridge, the site for the Robert Waller novel
and movie, *The Bridges of Madison County*. The bridge takes travelers north to Winterset,
Iowa, which is John Wayne's birthplace and the county seat.
Scout_____ Date _____ Tel_____ E-mail _____

NORTHEAST IOWA Dubuque, IA **Type** U **Issue** 9/94 **OA** Timmeu #74
Description: This patch shows the double-decked paddlewheeler, the "Spirit of Dubuque."
The riverboat symbolizes the Mississippi River's role as a great shipping route and
Dubuque's renown as a shipbuilding center (1850 to 1920). It also stresses the river's influ-
ence on the Council's service area. Today, this mode of transportation is still used on the
Mississippi River, and riverboat gambling is once again a popular diversion.
Scout_____ Date _____ Tel_____ E-mail _____

WINNEBAGO Waterloo, IA **Type** R **Issue** _____ **OA** Sac-N-Fox #108
Description: The peace pipe, or calumet, pictured was chosen as this Council's symbol when
the Mason City and Waterloo Councils merged in 1972. The name Winnebago was chosen
to commemorate the Native Americans who were indigenous to the area. Every March, this
Council also issues a special yearly CSP. Waterloo, Iowa, was known as Prairie Rapids
Crossing until 1851. The city plays host to the popular National Cattle Congress Exposi-
tion, an annual event.
Scout_____ Date _____ Tel_____ E-mail _____

N   M

CORONADO AREA Salina, KS **Type** U **Issue** _____ **OA** Kidi Kidish #434
Description: Pictured, is the Spanish explorer, Coronado. He gazes west across the rolling plains of Kansas at a prairie sunset. In 1541, he reached the Council territory looking for "Quivira." The legendary city of Quivira was purported to be a city of great riches, populated by very tall people. In actuality, it was a Wichita Native American village. This Council is located in central Kansas. In 1858, an antislavery group founded the city of Salina. Gigantic storage tanks and a large flourmill dot the city's landscape marking Salina's place as a noted trade and distribution center for hard wheat.
Scout_____ Date _____ Tel_____ E-mail _____

JAYHAWK AREA Topeka, KS **Type** U **Issue** '89 **OA** Dzie-Hauk Tonga #429
Description: This Council's headquarters is located in the state capital of Topeka. In 1971, the Jayhawk Council was the second in the nation (the first was Quivira) to switch to a colored Council patch. Designed in 1989, by Jay Stires, the current patch shows Jimmy Jayhawk. Although the exact meaning of the term "Jayhawk"is in dispute, it is used today as a nickname for all Kansans. The Jayhawk logo is used by both Kansas University and the Jayhawk Area Council.
Scout_____ Date _____ Tel_____ E-mail _____

QUIVIRA Wichita, KS **Type** N **Issue** '99 **OA** Kansa #198
Description: This Council is starting the year 2000 with a brand new CSP. The patch was based on a design by Michael Cartmill. The design represents the past, present, and future of the Council. The center of the patch features the "Keeper of the Plains," a south central Kansas icon, which represents the Council area's Native American heritage. The CSP's gold wheat field represents the fabled destination of Coronado, the "City of Gold." Pictured is the sunflower, the state flower. The airplane symbolizes the importance of aviation and space to the region's economy. The seven starred "Big Dipper" constellation, plus the North Star represent the Council's eight districts. The North Star further serves as a reminder of the Council's fixed purpose of serving the area's youth.
Scout_____ Date _____ Tel_____ E-mail _____

SANTA FE TRAIL Garden City, KS **Type** U **Issue** 1/96 **OA** Mandan #372
Description: Pictured on this CSP is a prairie schooner traveling on the 175 year old Santa Fe Trail, heading west to Walsenburg County, Kansas. The Council's high adventure camp, Spanish Peaks Scout Ranch, is located in Walsenburg. The Santa Fe Trail crosses Kansas from its northeast to the southwest corner. The trail was a major trade route from 1821 to 1880, and was in constant use. The river is the Cimarron River, a small tributary of the Arkansas River. It runs along the Santa Fe Trail and represents the Cimarron River District. The grazing buffalo symbolizes the Buffalo Range and the High Plains Districts.
Scout_____ Date _____ Tel_____ E-mail _____

V M

BLUE GRASS Lexington, KY **Type** U **Issue** '98 **OA** Kawida #480
Description: This new patch, designed by Andrew Lee, depicts Kentucky pictured in green, light-gray, and gray-purple. The Council's territory is also represented by the gray-purple region. The area is the country's main producer of bluegrass seed, hence the Council's name and Kentucky's nickname, "the Bluegrass State." The horse with rider represents the horse industry and the area's many horse farms and race tracks. The coon skin cap and the gunpowder horn symbolize Daniel Boone and the exploring he did here during pioneer days.
Scout_____ Date _____ Tel_____ E-mail _____

LINCOLN HERITAGE Louisville, KY **Type** N **Issue** 3/92 **OA** Talligewi #62
Description: This patch depicts Abraham Lincoln and a log cabin. When Old Kentucky Home Council, Ky., and George Rogers Clark Council, In., merged, Abraham Lincoln was one thing both Councils held in common. Lincoln was born near Hodgenville, Kentucky. Knob Creek, the first boyhood home remembered by Abraham Lincoln, was in this area. He also spent some time as a youth in southern Indiana. Louisville is the home of Fort Knox. Here, the U.S. Gold Depository houses most of the countries gold reserve. The region is known for raising Thoroughbred horses and for the Kentucky Derby, held each year at Churchill Downs. The derby is the oldest continuous horse race in the U.S.
Scout_____ Date _____ Tel_____ E-mail _____

SHAWNEE TRAILS Owensboro, KY **Type** R **Issue** '99 **OA** White Horse #201
Description: This CSP's design remains the same, but the new issue features silver mylar letters and is surrounded by a silver mylar border. The Council covers areas in Tennessee, Kentucky, and Illinois. The Shawnee Trails' name honors the Shawnee Native Americans, who considered Kentucky their hunting grounds. They had no permanent settlement there, but traveled extensively throughout the state of Kentucky. Their hunting trails, particularly from western Kentucky to Shawneetown, Illinois, opened the west to European expansion. This patch depicts a Shawnee brave and his son watching the sun set over their land. The Council is home to The National Scouting Museum.
Scout_____ Date _____ Tel_____ E-mail _____

ATTAKAPAS Alexandria, LA **Type** N **Issue** ____ **OA** Ouxouiga #264
Description: This Council's name is derived from the name of a local Native American tribe. This CSP, designed by Bob Kennedy, depicts a scene on Lake Seary and features Camp Attakapas in the background. The buildings shown are the Adirondacks of Camp Attakapas. They are being restored in a camp improvement project. To the left of the Adirondacks are the mighty long-leaf pines that are found throughout the camp's grounds. The Council serves 5 parishes in Central Louisiana: Allen, Avoyelles, Rapides, La Salle, and Grant.
Scout_____ Date _____ Tel_____ E-mail _____

CALCASIEU AREA Lake Charles, LA **Type** U **Issue** '98 **OA** Quelqueshoe #166
Description: This patch features the state bird—the brown pelican, a pine tree—representing the area's camping as well as Calcasieu Parish's renown as a leading lumber-producing region, and Louisiana with the Council's territory marked by a yellow star. The Scouting fleur-de-lis takes off, just as a space shuttle does, heading towards the future of Scouting. The Council's name means "Seeing Eagle" in Quequeshoe Native American. Their OA lodge also honors these people. The Lake Charles area is a deep-water port linked to the Gulf of Mexico by Lake Charles and the Calcasieu River in Cajun country. The "Gentleman Pirate," Jean Lafitte, was rumored to have hidden his treasures along the lake's shores.
Scout_____ Date _____ Tel_____ E-mail _____

EVANGELINE AREA Lafayette, LA **Type** U **Issue** '92 **OA** Atchafalaya #563
Description: This Council's patch represents the Cajun culture of southern Louisiana, particularly the eight-parish area called Acadiana. The oil industry, very important to the state's economy, is represented by an oil well. An alligator represents the swamplands of southern Louisiana. The crawfish, which looks like a small Maine lobster and is unique to southern Louisiana, is also shown. Crawfish or "Crawdaddys" are a tasty delicacy that has created a profitable industry for this area. The black iron pot represents the region's wonderful Cajun cuisine, like gumbo and jambalaya. The oak tree represents the many live oak trees across Louisiana's landscape and symbolizes Henry Wadsworth Longfellow's story, *Evangeline*.
Scout_____ Date _____ Tel_____ E-mail _____

ISTROUMA AREA Baton Rouge, LA **Type** U **Issue** ____ **OA** Quinipissa #479
Description: This unusual patch depicts the hills of Avondale in green. On the hill's right side can be found a cutout in the shape of a deer's head. The left hill contains a cutout of the Scout fleur-de-lis. This Council is located in the capital of Louisiana, Baton Rouge (French for "Red Stick"). The Council's name, Istrouma, also translates to "Red Stick" from the local Native American language. "Red Stick" refers to the Native American tradition of marking a tall cypress tree with fresh animal blood to mark the boundary between two tribes' hunting grounds.
Scout_____ Date _____ Tel_____ E-mail _____

NORWELA Shreveport, LA **Type** U **Issue** '91 **OA** Caddo #149
Description: This Council's name is an acronym for North West Louisiana. The patch pictures a paddle wheel steamboat on the Red River with the words "… All Ahead Full…," the motto of this Council's Scouting program. Prior to 1833, a logjam had dammed 165 miles of the river leaving it dry. Captain Henry Miller Shreve restarted the river, and thus the economy, flowing. Shreveport was named in his honor. Each April, Shreveport hosts the Holiday in Dixie festival commemorating the Louisiana Purchase of 1803.
Scout_____ Date _____ Tel_____ E-mail _____

N

A

B

OUACHITA VALLEY Monroe, LA **Type** N **Issue** '85 **OA** Comanche #254
Description: This Council's name is from the Ouachita Native Americans. The CSP shows
a deer—the totem of the Council's OA lodge, and an old oak tree found in the middle of the
Council's Scout camp. The area is the trade center for northeast Louisiana. The city of Mon-
roe was named for the James Monroe, the first steamboat to travel up the Ouachita River.
Scout_____ Date _____ Tel_____ E-mail _____

SOUTHEAST LOUISIANA Metairie, LA **Type** R **Issue** '99 **OA** Chilantakoba #397
Description: This is the new name for the former New Orleans Area Council. The name
change better represents the parishes (counties) now served by the Council. The bird in the
foreground is the state bird and OA lodge totem, the pelican. The flying ducks denote the
area's diversity of wildlife. The cypress trees pictured are found throughout the state. The
body of water symbolizes the Mississippi Gulf Coast, Lake Pontchartrain, and the area's
many bayous. New Orleans is a port city, most of which is located below sea level. The
shining sun represents a new age for the area's Scouting program. Southeast Louisiana, from
its Creole and Cajun restaurants, to New Orleans' French Quarter—home of Jazz and its
Garden District—home of Tulane and Loyola Universities, to the region's many festivals,
plantation homes, and of course, Mardi Gras,has something for everyone.
Scout_____ Date _____ Tel_____ E-mail _____

KATAHDIN AREA Bangor, ME **Type** U **Issue** '79 **OA** Pamola #211
Description: This patch depicts Mt. Katahdin found in Baxter State Park. The mountain's
highest summit is the 5,268-foot Baxter Peak, the highest point in Maine. The park contains
the northern end of the Appalachian Trail. Also shown are the coast of Maine, potato fields
and pine forests. The potato fields represent northeast Maine's importance as a potato-farm-
ing region. The white pine tree is the state tree. Lumbering was a major industry here in
the 19th century.
Scout_____ Date _____ Tel_____ E-mail _____

PINE TREE Portland, ME **Type** N **Issue** '99 **OA** Madockawanda #271
Description: This Council has returned to its previously designed patch. The Council's
name refers to Maine's nickname, "the Pine Tree State." Most of its territory is covered by
white pines, the state tree. The state flower is the white pine cone and tassel. Maine is also
well known for its many lighthouses. The lighthouse shown can be seen in Casco Bay, home
of the "Calendar Islands," so named because there are 365 islands. Two Lights State Park
is nearby as well. Portland is the birthplace of the poet Henry Wadsworth Longfellow author
of such works as *Evangeline* (1847), *The Song of Hiawatha* (1855), and *Tales of a Wayside
Inn* (1863), which contains the popular poem, "Paul Revere's Ride." His childhood home,
in Portland, is now a museum.
Scout_____ Date _____ Tel_____ E-mail _____

M

M

BALTIMORE AREA Baltimore, MD **Type** U **Issue** 5/95 **OA** Nentico #12
Description: The red crab represents the steamed crab, which is a regional specialty. The
Baltimore Oriole symbolizes both the state bird and Baltimore Orioles baseball team. The
sailing ship is the Constellation, presently berthed in Baltimore Harbor. Also pictured is the
Baltimore skyline, symbolic of the revitalized city vicinity. The Inner Harbor area of the
city features a park, hotels, and Harbor Place—the waterfront shopping and restaurant dis-
trict. Some of Baltimore's places of interest include the home and grave of writer Edgar
Allan Poe; Fort McHenry National Monument—inspiration for Francis Scott Key's "The
Star Spangled Banner;" and the birthplace of baseball great, Babe Ruth.
Scout_____ Date _____ Tel_____ E-mail _____
MASON-DIXON Hagerstown, MD **Type** N **Issue** ____ **OA** Guneukitschik #317
Description: The imaginary Mason-Dixon line, which divided slave states from free states
during the Civil War, was the inspiration for this Council's name. Surveyors Charles Mason
and Jeremiah Dixon established the line from 1763 to 1767. The patch is blue and gray, the
colors of the northern and southern troops, respectively. Also featured are the BSA fleur-
de-lis and the flags of the Confederate States and the United States of America. This design
represents the unity that exists between these once warring states and among all Boy Scouts.
Scout_____ Date _____ Tel_____ E-mail _____
NATIONAL CAPITAL AREA Bethesda, MD **Type** U **Issue** '74
                                                        OA Amagamek-Wipit #470
Description: This National Capital Area CSP, in use since 1974, features the Jefferson
Memorial. The memorial, located along the Potomac River's Tidal Basin, was completed
in 1943. It honors our third president and founding father, Thomas Jefferson. The Memo-
rial houses a bronze statue of Jefferson and the walls are inscribed with some of his famous
quotes. Also pictured are the beautiful cherry blossoms for which our nation's capital is
famous. These trees, of the Oriental and Nanking varieties, were a gift from Japan in 1912.
The Council serves youth in parts of Maryland, Washington, DC, and Virginia.
Scout_____ Date _____ Tel_____ E-mail _____
POTOMAC Cumberland, MD **Type** U **Issue** ____ **OA** Ahtuhquog #540
Description: The Potomac Council serves two counties in Maryland and four counties in
West Virginia. This is represented by the outline of the two states in black. Also shown is
George Washington who, in his younger days, often surveyed in this area. In 1787, during
the French and Indian War, the 21-year-old Washington was headquartered at Fort Cumber-
land. The Council's name is from the Potomac Native Americans who lived in the region.
The Potomacs were one of the 30 bands of Algonquians which formed the Powhatan Con-
federacy. The Potomac River is part of the boundary between West Virginia and Maryland.
Scout_____ Date _____ Tel_____ E-mail _____

M

ANNAWON Taunton, MA **Type** U **Issue** mid-1960's **OA** Tulpe #245
Description: This patch, designed by Frederick Govain, features Chief Annawon (Commander), the chief military strategist during King Philip's War (1675). The uprising protested the Pilgrim's increasing demands for Native American land. Annawon was forced to hide in a swamp near Taunton. He was later captured and behead. His motto was "Ioutash," which translates into "Stand Firm." The red and blue represents the two districts that make up this Council. The Council serves eleven towns and cities in southeastern Massachusetts.
Scout_____ Date _____ Tel_____ E-mail _____

BOSTON MINUTEMAN Boston, MA **Type** R **Issue** ____ **OA** Moswetuset #52
Description: This CSP depicts the area's history. It was designed by Michael A.Caristinos. Pictured are the Liberty Tree and a Concord Minuteman, for which this Council was named. He is crossing the Old North Bridge, the site of "The Shot Heard 'round the World," which started the American Revolution. Minutemen were patriotic civilians of Massachusetts and other New England colonies. Before the Revolution, they volunteered to fight the British at a minute's notice, thus their name. Paul Revere is seen riding, warning that the British were coming. The moon and dark blue sky remind us of that historic midnight ride. Boston's skyline, with its interesting combination of old and new buildings, is also depicted.
Scout_____ Date _____ Tel_____ E-mail _____

CAMBRIDGE Cambridge, MA **Type** N **Issue** '87 **OA** Kahagon #131
Description: This CSP honors Cambridge's many fine universities. The city is home to Harvard (the oldest college in the U.S.), Massachusetts Institute of Technology (MIT), and Radcliff. The two stars encircled in green represent service stars that were earned as a Boy Scout. The stars also represent the Scouting program's ideals of truth and knowledge. Cambridge Commons is the site where, in 1775, George Washington took command of the Continental Army.
Scout_____ Date _____ Tel_____ E-mail _____

CAPE COD & ISLANDS Yarmouth, MA **Type** R **Issue** '96
                                            OA Abake Mi-Sa-Na-Ki #393
Description: This CSP was designed by Ed Mathews. The lighthouse shown is similar to Nantucket Lighthouse and is indicative of six others found in the region. The water pictured represents the Atlantic Ocean, Cape Cod Bay, and Nantucket Sound. The tall sailboat stresses the region's renown as a tourist area, summer resort, and fishing ground. English explorer Bartholomew Gosnold named the region Cape Cod due to the area's abundance of codfish. The whale symbolizes the area's history as a great whaling port during the 18th century. Within the Council's territory are the Cape Cod National Seashore, Martha's Vineyard, and Nantucket Island, all popular summer tourist stops.
Scout_____ Date _____ Tel_____ E-mail _____

M   N

GREAT TRAILS Dalton, MA **Type** N **Issue** '95 **OA** Memsochet #507
Description: This CSP was designed by Joe Csatari, official artist for the BSA. It reflects
the local historical landmarks and the region's Native American history. The "Great Trails"
are the Mohawk, Appalachian, and Nonotuck Trails in western Massachusetts. The profiles
of the three indians represent the three tribes that inhabited the area. When in Dalton, dis-
cover the history of American papermaking by touring the Crane Museum of Papermaking.
Scout_____ Date _____ Tel_____ E-mail _____

KNOX TRAIL Framingham, MA **Type** U **Issue** '98 **OA** Chippanyonk #59
Description: This Council, honoring General Henry Knox, was born in 1996 from the merger of Algonquin and Norumbega Councils, represented on the CSP by the two fleurs-de-lis.
It was designed by Jim Chesna, Camp Ranger. The "BSA" symbolizes Knox's winding trail
through both former Councils, tying them together as one. The black silhouette depicts General Knox inspecting his "Noble Train of Artillery," which traveled via sled through winter
weather from Fort Ticonderoga, N.Y., to Cambridge and Dorchester Heights, Massachusetts.
The flag to the left is the "Grand Union" or "Cambridge" flag, which was flown by George
Washington over Cambridge in January, 1776. The flag on the right was the British Naval
Ensign. The white background represents the snow of the winter of 1775-1776. The gold
border signifies the circle of friendship and the bright future of the Knox Trail Council. The
OA name means, "Where the Tribes Assemble."
Scout_____Date _____ Tel_____ E-mail _____

MOBY DICK New Bedford, MA **Type** U **Issue** ____ **OA** Neemat #124
Description: This Council's territory is rich in whaling and shipbuilding history. The CSP
displays the Atlantic Ocean and Buzzards Bay, a tall ship, a battleship, and a white whale.
The whale represents *Moby Dick; or, The White Whale* (1851), Herman Melville's riveting
novel. The New Bedford Whaling Museum offers visitors a chance to board a fully rigged
half model of the Lagoda, a whaling ship, similar to the ship depicted on this patch. The
battleship pictured is the USS Massachusetts, which is berthed in nearby Fall River.
Scout_____Date _____ Tel_____ E-mail _____

MOHEGAN Worcester, MA **Type** R **Issue** '99 **OA** Pachachaug #525
Description: This new CSP features the profile of a Mohegan emblazoned with a fleur-de-
lis. The Council is named for the Mohegan Native Americans indigenous to this area in the
before the 1700's. The center design is a BSA logo within a compass. The points of the
compass direct us to the concepts important in Scouting—strong values, strong leaders, and
character counts (the 1997 National Jamboree motto). The icon at the right is taken from
the Massachusetts state flag and state seal. A major attraction of the region is Old Sturbridge
Historic Village, a re-creation of a 1790-1840 New England community.
Scout_____Date _____ Tel_____ E-mail _____

Massachusetts

A

NASHUA VALLEY Lancaster, MA **Type** N **Issue** 6/93 **OA** Grand Monadnock #309
Description: The Nashua Valley Council name honors the Nashaway Native Americans who
lived in the area. The patch design represents the many little white churches, the covered
bridges, red maple trees, and the farm houses that are abundant throughout the Council's
rural communities. The Council is situated between the Watatic and Wachusetts Mountains.
To the north lies Grand Monadnock Mountain, New Hampshire, for which the OA lodge was
named. Grand Monadnock Mountain is the second most climbed mountain in the world.
Scout_____Date _____ Tel_____ E-mail _____

OLD COLONY Canton, MA **Type** R **Issue** '83 **OA** Tisquantum #164
Description: This Council's name and patch honor the first colonists that settled in the Ply-
mouth area (1620). "Old Colony" was the original name the Pilgrims gave to the region.
The ship is a representation of one of the more historic Pilgrim ships, the Mayflower. The
Council's attractions include a full-size replica similar to the original Mayflower, Plymouth
Rock, and Plimoth Plantation. The Council serves Bristol, Plymouth, and Norfolk counties.
Scout_____Date _____ Tel_____ E-mail _____

PIONEER VALLEY Chicopee, MA **Type** U **Issue** _____ **OA** Allogagan #83
Description: Reflected on this CSP are the many famous products that were first produced
within this Council's service area. The plane is a "GB," a famous racing plane manufactured here, symbolic of the region's aircraft-engine industry and Westover Air Force Base.
The rifle is the Springfield rifle made in the area in 1903, as was the Remington Sword on
the patch. The ball represents the game of basketball, which was first started here in Springfield. Basketball was invented, in 1891, by Dr. James Naismith, a physical education teacher
at the School for Christian Workers. Springfield, Massachusetts is also home to the National Basketball Hall of Fame. In addition, Chicopee (Native American, "Birch Bark Place")
is a large manufacturing center for sporting goods and inflatable rubber products. The blue
water represents the Connecticut River. The green mountain is Mount Tom.
Scout_____Date _____ Tel_____ E-mail _____

YANKEE CLIPPER Haverhill, MA **Type** R **Issue** _____ **OA** Nanepashemet #158
Description: This Council's name and CSP honors the "Yankee Clipper" ships. Clippers
were used during the 1850's to carry cargo across the seas. The ships had a reputation for
being very fast vessels, and they set many long-enduring speed records. The blue waters of
the Atlantic Ocean lie at the patch's bottom. The ship's wheel and the compass points further stress the importance of the area's waterways for trade, transportation, fishing, and
recreation. Haverhill was also a major shipbuilding center from the 1690's to 1815. This
Council serves boys in parts of Massachusetts and New Hampshire.
Scout_____Date _____ Tel_____ E-mail _____

BLUE WATER Port Huron, MI **Type** U **Issue** 9/97 **OA** Chickagami #180
Description: This Council serves areas in S.E. Michigan (Sanilac and St. Clair Counties) along the St.Clair River between Lake Huron and Lake Erie. "Blue Water" refers to Lake Huron and the St. Clair River. The CSP depicts the water's brilliant clear blue color, which is attributed to the lack of silt and dirt in Lake Huron. A freighter is shown carrying cargo down the St. Clair. Lake Huron is a center for commercial travel and a haven for many recreational activities. It handles more traffic than the Panama and Suez Canals combined. Pictured is the Blue Water International Bridge, one of three bridges that connects the U.S. with Canada. A new span, added in 1997, was opened by a parade of 200,000 people walking across it, led by U.S. and Canadian Scouts. Port Huron is the boyhood home of inventor Thomas Alva Edison. This CSP was designed by Jeffrey Kunnath.
Scout_____ Date _____ Tel_____ E-mail _____

CHIEF OKEMOS Lansing, MI **Type** U **Issue** '70 **OA** Gabe-Shi-Win-Gi-Ji-Kens #374
Description: Chief Okemos Council is named for Native American Chief Okemos, who, it is believed, is buried on the Council's camp property. Since the Council is located in Michigan's capital city, Lansing, the patch features the State Capitol Building, completed in 1878. The rays radiating from the capitol signify Scouting's influence in the tri-county area. Some of the region's sites include the hands-on Impression 5 Science Center, the R. E. Olds Transportation Museum (Oldsmobile autos), and Michigan State University.
Scout_____ Date _____ Tel_____ E-mail _____

CLINTON VALLEY Pontiac, MI **Type** U **Issue** '99 **OA** Chippewa #29
Description: The Council's name is derived from the valley around the Clinton River near Detroit. This colorful new patch was designed by Program Director, Kevin Nichols. The Scout Sign is pictured mid-patch. The three raised fingers represent the three parts of the Scout Oath. The thumb and pinky touch in a symbol of unity with all Scouts throughout the world. The Council is headquartered in Pontiac, Michigan, which is named for the famous Chief Pontiac (Ottawa). A statute commemorating the chief stands in the lobby of City Hall.
Scout_____ Date _____ Tel_____ E-mail _____

DETROIT AREA Detroit, MI **Type** U **Issue** ____ **OA** Mi-Gi-Si O-Paw-Gan #162
Description: This patch features Detroit's majestic skyline. The tall rectangular buildings are the Renaissance Center, part of the city's revitalized downtown area. The Great Lakes freighter represents Detroit's position as a port of entry on the Detroit River and its location connecting the upper and lower Great Lakes. The fleur-de-lis with the American eagle in the center is proudly displayed . Detroit, Michigan's largest city, has earned the nickname "The Motor City" due to its status as the world's leading automobile manufacturing center. The city is also the home of the "Motown" sound, a rhythm-and-blues music style.
Scout_____ Date _____ Tel_____ E-mail _____

Michigan

GERALD R. FORD Grand Rapids, MI **Type** N **Issue** 2/92 **OA** Nacha Tindey #25
Description: Gerald R. Ford Council honors our 38th President. Ford lived in Grand Rapids from childhood to college age. The city is home to The Ford Presidential Museum. The deer and pine trees symbolize the abundant wildlife, rural areas, outdoor experiences of Scouting, and the Council's Camp Gerber. The blue water represents Lake Michigan and other regional lakes. An eagle soars, as the sun rises on Scouting. Area landmarks include the 43-foot high metal sculpture by Alexander Calder, "La Grande Vitesse," (Vitesse means "rapids" in French) and the Fish Ladder Sculpture, which was built to aid salmon over a 6-foot dam on their way to their spawning grounds.
Scout_____ Date _____ Tel_____ E-mail _____

GREAT SAUK TRAIL Ann Arbor, MI **Type** N **Issue** 1/94 **OA** Manitous #88
Description: The Sauk Trail is the name given to the "trail" which winds through the forests of southern Michigan. The trail, forged by Native Americans, was also well traveled by French trappers and traders and the British military. The wagon wheel symbolizes colonial use of the road. In the 1820's, the trail became the second U.S. road (now U.S. 12). Shown is chief Baw Beese, of the Potawatomi ("People of the Place of Fire" in Algonquin). Baw Beese and his people are remembered for befriending and aiding the English settlers. Eventually, Baw Beese and 200 of his people were forced onto a reservation north of Topeka, Kansas. His descendants still live there today. On this patch, a Scout can be seen traveling the Sauk Trail, just as he travels his own advancement trail through Scouting.
Scout_____ Date _____ Tel_____ E-mail _____

HIAWATHALAND Marquette, MI **Type** U **Issue** '96 **OA** Ag-Im #156
Description: This Council covers most of the Upper Peninsula of Michigan "the Great Lakes State," and a part of Wisconsin as well. It was named for Henry Wadsworth Longfellow's fictional Hiawatha and the shores of Gitche-Gumme (Lake Superior). The blue water represents the surrounding Great Lakes. The canoe and Indian represent the area's rich Native American heritage. The glowing campfire symbolizes fellowship in Scouting and the Council's camping program. The trees also symbolize camping and focus on the region's large forestry industry. The sun spreads its rays and warmth throughout the Council's area.
Scout_____ Date _____ Tel_____ E-mail _____

LAKE HURON AREA Auburn, MI **Type** U **Issue** ____ **OA** Mischigonong #89
Description: This Council is named for the second largest of the Great Lakes, Lake Huron. The Huron Native Americans (Iroquoian family) were early inhabitants of the region. The area's beauty and peacefulness is symbolized by the soaring sea gull, white clouds, tall pine trees, purple waters, and blue skies. Lower Michigan is represented by the map-like shape. The yellow denotes the Council's service area, and the fleur-de-lis marks their headquarters.
Scout_____ Date _____ Tel_____ E-mail _____

A

SCENIC TRAILS Traverse City, MI **Type** U **Issue** _____ **OA** Indian Drum #152
Description: This CSP's name and patch represent the numerous trails and walking paths that are in the 13 counties which comprise this Council. In addition to the blue skies, tall trees, green grasslands, and brown earthen paths, the state of Michigan is pictured in red and white. The white area, with the Council's number "274," symbolizes the region this Council serves. Traverse City was once a lumber milling town. When the trees were exhausted, the town became a flourishing cherry growing region.
Scout_____ Date _____ Tel_____ E-mail _____

SOUTHWEST MICHIGAN Kalamazoo, MI **Type** U **Issue** '91 **OA** Nacha-Mawat #373
Description: This patch was designed by Ronald L. Kirshman and chosen via a contest in 1991. It features the bronze statue of "The Scout" on the wooden walkway, above the fire bowl at Camp Rota-Kiwan. Kalamazoo, the Council's headquarters, means "Place Where the Water Boils" in Native American. It refers to the many bubbling springs found in the area's riverbeds. The Council area plays host to several special events such as the Kalamazoo Kitefest (April), The World's Longest Breakfast Table (June), the Battle Creek International Balloon Fest (July), the Kalamazoo County Flowerfest (mid-July), the Michigan Wine and Harvest Festival (one week after Labor Day), and the New Year's Fest. Battle Creek, Mi., is the headquarter city of the Kellogg., Post, and Ralston Purina Companies. Abolitionist and women's rights activist Sojourner Truth is buried in Battle Creek.
Scout_____ Date _____ Tel_____ E-mail _____

TALL PINE Flint, MI **Type** U **Issue** _____ **OA** Cuwe #218
Description: This CSP speaks of the area's great history. Michigan appears in yellow and the red represents the Council's area. The tall pine tree symbolizes the OA lodge's totem, the region's natural resources, and the area's fame as a vehicle-assembling region. In the 1800's, Flint was a large lumbering center, with its sawmills providing materials for carriage and wagon manufacturers. In 1908, General Motors began and chose Flint as its national headquarters, thus establishing the city's reputation as a major motor vehicle assembling area. The city has been nicknamed "Vehicle City." The name Flint comes from the Native American name given to the river, Pawanunling, meaning "River of Flint."
Scout_____ Date _____ Tel_____ E-mail _____

CENTRAL MINNESOTA St. Cloud, MN **Type** U **Issue** 1/94 **OA** Naguonabe #31
Description: This patch's design represents the lake country of central Minnesota. Depicted are images of ducks and geese (the state bird is the common loon, and the region is a part of the Mississippi Flyway), woodlands (the area is a large paper products and Christmas tree producer), and a canoe on a lake (Minnesota is nicknamed the "Land of 10,000 Lakes"). The Sioux word "Minnesota" means "Cloudy Water."
Scout_____ Date _____ Tel_____ E-mail _____

Minnesota
M, A

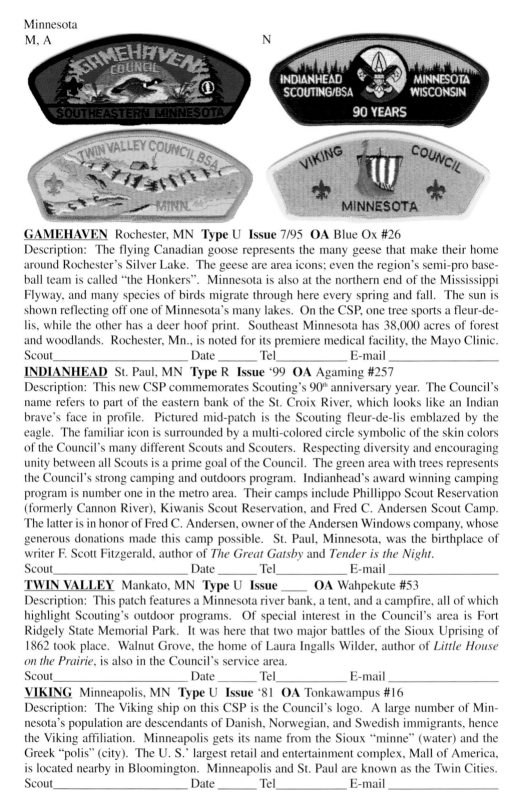

GAMEHAVEN Rochester, MN **Type** U **Issue** 7/95 **OA** Blue Ox #26
Description: The flying Canadian goose represents the many geese that make their home around Rochester's Silver Lake. The geese are area icons; even the region's semi-pro baseball team is called "the Honkers". Minnesota is also at the northern end of the Mississippi Flyway, and many species of birds migrate through here every spring and fall. The sun is shown reflecting off one of Minnesota's many lakes. On the CSP, one tree sports a fleur-de-lis, while the other has a deer hoof print. Southeast Minnesota has 38,000 acres of forest and woodlands. Rochester, Mn., is noted for its premiere medical facility, the Mayo Clinic.
Scout_____ Date _____ Tel_____ E-mail _____

INDIANHEAD St. Paul, MN **Type** R **Issue** '99 **OA** Agaming #257
Description: This new CSP commemorates Scouting's 90th anniversary year. The Council's name refers to part of the eastern bank of the St. Croix River, which looks like an Indian brave's face in profile. Pictured mid-patch is the Scouting fleur-de-lis emblazed by the eagle. The familiar icon is surrounded by a multi-colored circle symbolic of the skin colors of the Council's many different Scouts and Scouters. Respecting diversity and encouraging unity between all Scouts is a prime goal of the Council. The green area with trees represents the Council's strong camping and outdoors program. Indianhead's award winning camping program is number one in the metro area. Their camps include Phillippo Scout Reservation (formerly Cannon River), Kiwanis Scout Reservation, and Fred C. Andersen Scout Camp. The latter is in honor of Fred C. Andersen, owner of the Andersen Windows company, whose generous donations made this camp possible. St. Paul, Minnesota, was the birthplace of writer F. Scott Fitzgerald, author of *The Great Gatsby* and *Tender is the Night*.
Scout_____ Date _____ Tel_____ E-mail _____

TWIN VALLEY Mankato, MN **Type** U **Issue** ____ **OA** Wahpekute #53
Description: This patch features a Minnesota river bank, a tent, and a campfire, all of which highlight Scouting's outdoor programs. Of special interest in the Council's area is Fort Ridgely State Memorial Park. It was here that two major battles of the Sioux Uprising of 1862 took place. Walnut Grove, the home of Laura Ingalls Wilder, author of *Little House on the Prairie*, is also in the Council's service area.
Scout_____ Date _____ Tel_____ E-mail _____

VIKING Minneapolis, MN **Type** U **Issue** '81 **OA** Tonkawampus #16
Description: The Viking ship on this CSP is the Council's logo. A large number of Minnesota's population are descendants of Danish, Norwegian, and Swedish immigrants, hence the Viking affiliation. Minneapolis gets its name from the Sioux "minne" (water) and the Greek "polis" (city). The U. S.' largest retail and entertainment complex, Mall of America, is located nearby in Bloomington. Minneapolis and St. Paul are known as the Twin Cities.
Scout_____ Date _____ Tel_____ E-mail _____

VOYAGEURS AREA Hermantown, MN **Type** U **Issue** 12/94

OA Ka'Niss Ma'Ingan #196

Description: This Council serves parts of Minnesota, Wisconsin, and Michigan. On this CSP, the canoe and people in the canoe depict the first non-Native American voyageurs (French-Canadian trappers and pioneers) that came to explore northern Minnesota and northern Wisconsin in the 1600's. The river and forest represent the Council's environment and Voyageurs National Park. The park, formed in 1975, consists of more than one-third water. A park visitor can spot moose, black bear, deer, timber wolves, and many types of fish. Nearby Duluth, located on Lake Superior, is the furthest inland seaport of the Great Lakes.

Scout_____ Date _____ Tel_____ E-mail _____

ANDREW JACKSON Jackson, MS **Type** U **Issue** ____ **OA** Sebooney Okasucca #260

Description: This Council's territory includes Mississippi's largest city and state capital, Jackson. Both the city (1822) and the Council were named in honor of Andrew Jackson, famous general, lawyer, congressman, senator, and seventh president of the United States (1829). The CSP's background is the Mississippi state flag. The gray border represents Mississippi's place as part of the southern Confederacy. The shape of the state and the Council's area are found on the map, set into the yellow fleur-de-lis. During the American Civil War, Jackson, Ms., was burned to the ground by Union Troops. The city's charred appearance gave it the nickname, "Chimneyville."

Scout_____ Date _____ Tel_____ E-mail _____

CHOCTAW AREA Meridian, MS **Type** U **Issue** ____ **OA** Ashwanchi Kinta #193

Description: Pictured in a canoe is a Choctaw Native American. This Council derives its name from the Choctaws, who inhabited the area. The patch's background is formed from the blending of the state flags of Mississippi (on the left) and Alabama (on the right). The CSP features Mississippi and Alabama in yellow. The Council's area is shown in white and represents the five Mississippi counties and the one Alabama county it serves. Meridian is home to a museum devoted to country singer Jimmie Rodgers.

Scout_____ Date _____ Tel_____ E-mail _____

PINE BURR AREA Hattiesburg, MS **Type** U **Issue** ____ **OA** Ti'ak #404

Description: This CSP, with its white background and red border, beautifully represents the Council's heritage. The Mississippi River is seen flowing through the patch, creating a waterway for the Native Americans (the red canoe), the shrimpers (the blue shrimp boat), and the sea gulls. The Mississippi also nourishes the cypress trees, shown with their hanging Spanish moss, and the tall green pine trees. The pine trees are also a reminder that the area is home to De Soto National Forest. A blue fleur-de-lis is pictured with the Mississippi state seal at its center.

Scout_____ Date _____ Tel_____ E-mail _____

M, A

V

PUSHMATAHA AREA Columbus, MS **Type** U **Issue** _____ **OA** Watonala #169
Description: This Council's name comes from Chief Pushmataha of the local Choctaw
Nation. He is featured on this CSP. Pushmataha, a peaceful man, was responsible for keeping many tribes from joining Chief Tecumseh's war against the white settlers. The Choctaws
along with the Cherokees, Creeks, Chickasaws, and Seminoles were known as the "Five Civilized Tribes." The Choctaw people were relocated from their land, beginning what is known
as the "Trail of Tears," the forced march of the Five Civilized Tribes. Pushmataha's grave
may be visited at Congressional Cemetery in Washington, DC. The tree behind the chief
has been struck by lightning, as was an old oak tree found at the Council's Camp Seminole.
On the right is the Mississippi state flag, and on the left is a generic BSA troop flag.
Scout_____ Date _____ Tel_____ E-mail _____

YOCONA AREA Tupelo, MS **Type** U **Issue** '98 **OA** Chicksa #202
Description: "Yocona" or "Yakni" is the Choctaw word for "earth." This patch shows two
types of Chickasaw lodges, and a Chickasaw warrior with a spear. The three soaring birds
represent the three spirits who helped the Chickasaws win all of their wars. A cornstalk,
crowned by a golden fleur-de-lis, represents corn, a staple of the Chickasaw's diet. Tupelo
is the site of the most sacred of the Chickasaw Indian mounds. Tupelo was known as "Old
Town" by the Chickasaws. The date on the patch, "1926," represents the beginning of the
Council. Elvis Presley, the "King of Rock 'n' Roll," was born in Tupelo on January 8, 1935.
Scout_____ Date _____ Tel_____ E-mail _____

GREAT RIVERS Columbia, MO **Type** U **Issue** '73 **OA** Nampa-Tsi #216
Description: The Mississippi and the Missouri are the "Great Rivers" of this Council. The
Mississippi creates the eastern boundary, while the Missouri bisects the Council's territory.
Pictured are the Missouri State Capitol in Jefferson City and a riverboat, a frequent river ves-
sel of olden days. Daniel Boone, an early explorer in the area, kneels on the riverbank. He
started the Boonslick Trail near Columbia, Mo., and a salt refinery at a nearby saline spring.
Scout_____ Date _____ Tel_____ E-mail _____

GREATER ST. LOUIS AREA St. Louis, MO **Type** U **Issue** _____ **OA** Shawnee #51
                                                                              Anpetu-We #100
Description: The famous stainless steel Gateway Arch is featured on this CSP. The arch,
designed by Eero Saarinen, is 650-feet high (75 feet taller than the Washington Monument)
and was completed in 1965. It is part of the Jefferson National Expansion Memorial National Historic Site. The Arch celebrates the city's role as the gateway to the American West for
19th century pioneers. St. Louis is also a gateway to Scouting for many of the area's boys.
The red and white clouds and blue border symbolize the bringing together of American West
under the U.S. flag. The blue water represents Illinois' Stripe River.
Scout_____ Date _____ Tel_____ E-mail _____

M   V, A

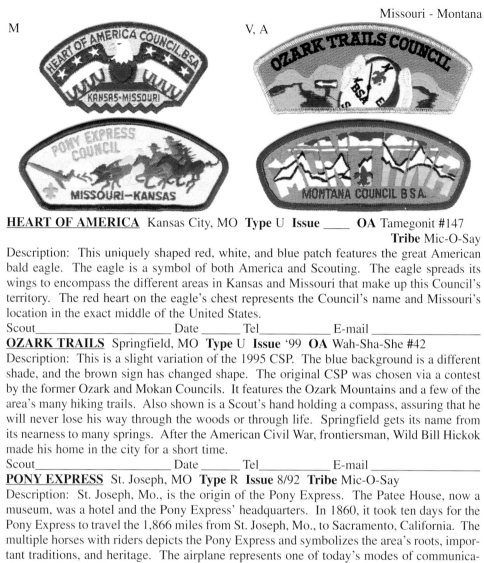

HEART OF AMERICA Kansas City, MO **Type** U **Issue** _____ **OA** Tamegonit #147
                                                          Tribe Mic-O-Say
Description: This uniquely shaped red, white, and blue patch features the great American bald eagle. The eagle is a symbol of both America and Scouting. The eagle spreads its wings to encompass the different areas in Kansas and Missouri that make up this Council's territory. The red heart on the eagle's chest represents the Council's name and Missouri's location in the exact middle of the United States.
Scout_____ Date _____ Tel_____ E-mail _____

OZARK TRAILS Springfield, MO **Type** U **Issue** '99 **OA** Wah-Sha-She #42
Description: This is a slight variation of the 1995 CSP. The blue background is a different shade, and the brown sign has changed shape. The original CSP was chosen via a contest by the former Ozark and Mokan Councils. It features the Ozark Mountains and a few of the area's many hiking trails. Also shown is a Scout's hand holding a compass, assuring that he will never lose his way through the woods or through life. Springfield gets its name from its nearness to many springs. After the American Civil War, frontiersman, Wild Bill Hickok made his home in the city for a short time.
Scout_____ Date _____ Tel_____ E-mail _____

PONY EXPRESS St. Joseph, MO **Type** R **Issue** 8/92 **Tribe** Mic-O-Say
Description: St. Joseph, Mo., is the origin of the Pony Express. The Patee House, now a museum, was a hotel and the Pony Express' headquarters. In 1860, it took ten days for the Pony Express to travel the 1,866 miles from St. Joseph, Mo., to Sacramento, California. The multiple horses with riders depicts the Pony Express and symbolizes the area's roots, important traditions, and heritage. The airplane represents one of today's modes of communication—airmail. It illustrates the Council's readiness to move into the future and its willingness to provide a forward-looking program in Scouting. When in "St. Joe" one may visit the Pony Express Museum. The city also has the distinction of being the place where outlaw Jesse James was killed by his own gang member for a $10,000 reward (1882).
Scout_____ Date _____ Tel_____ E-mail _____

MONTANA Great Falls, MT **Type** U **Issue** _____ **OA** Apoxky Aio #300
Description: The word "Montana" means "mountainous" in Spanish. When Lewis and Clark's expedition arrived in 1805, they encountered the Blackfoot Native Americans. The Lewis and Clark National Forest commemorates this event. The city of Great Falls still has a large Native American population. The city's name reflects its location near the falls of the Missouri River. Giant Springs, one of the world's largest freshwater springs, is also nearby. This patch has the name of the state, "Montana," embroidered on it. Each letter features a sunset peeking out from behind the mountains.
Scout_____ Date _____ Tel_____ E-mail _____

M,

CORNHUSKER Lincoln, NE **Type** U **Issue** _____ **OA** Golden Sun #492
Description: Nebraska is corn country, and this is beautifully depicted by both this Council's patch and name. Cornhusker is also the name of the University of Nebraska's football team. Corn is the major crop of the region, with 75 percent of Nebraska's irrigated land devoted to its growth. The patch's scene represents the abundance of farmhouses, cornfields, and sun that are found throughout the Council's territory. The Council is located in the capital of Nebraska, Lincoln, named in honor of President Abraham Lincoln.
Scout_____ Date _____ Tel_____ E-mail _____

MID-AMERICA Omaha, NE **Type** R **Issue** _____ **OA** Kit-Ke-Hak-O-Kut #97
Description: Prairie Gold Area Council has joined this Council as of May 2000. Their patch features an all-American theme represented by the prominent American bald eagle within the Council's red, white, and blue initials. The Council incorporates areas in Nebraska and Iowa and is located at what is almost the geographical center of the United States. Omaha is the largest city in Nebraska. It is named for one of the region's Native American tribes and means "Upstream People." The famous landmark trial, Standing Bear vs. Crook, took place here in 1879. The verdict declared that Native Americans are to be treated as human beings under U.S. law. Boys Town is also nearby. Arbor Day, founded by Julius Sterling Morton (Morton Salt), was begun here in 1872.
Scout_____ Date _____ Tel_____ E-mail _____

OVERLAND TRAILS Grand Island, NE **Type** U **Issue** 1/94 **OA** Tatanka-Anpetu-Wi #94
Description: This patch represents the varied geography and history of the region. The tepees represent the Pawnee tribe. The wagon pulled by oxen symbolizes the area's pioneer heritage and the thousands of westward bound settlers who followed the region's trails. The buffalo and deer represent the animals that have inhabited the vicinity. The OA name means "buffalo sun." The buffalo is also their totem. To the left of the sun is a sandhill crane. The crane's spring migration bottlenecks the area when hundreds of thousands of birds descend on it. All these symbols sit on an island, just as this Council's camp does in the Platte River.
Scout_____ Date _____ Tel_____ E-mail _____

BOULDER DAM AREA Las Vegas, NV **Type** R **Issue** 6/94 **OA** Nebagamon #312
Description: This CSP features Boulder Dam, also known as Hoover Dam. Tim Gittus designed it with final artwork by Tish Hess. It embraces three themes. First is the flora of the area, which is mainly desert flowers with an occasional meadow. Las Vegas means "the Meadows" in Spanish. Second is gambling, Las Vegas' primary industry, represented by the silver dollars propped against the yucca trees. The third theme is Boulder Dam. The dam provides water and electricity to the area and adjoining states. The lightning bolts symbolize the power and energy that come from the dam and that Scouting gives to its members.
Scout_____ Date _____ Tel_____ E-mail _____

N, A

NEVADA AREA Reno, NV **Type** U **Issue** _____ **OA** Tannu #346
Description: This Council serves parts of Nevada and California. The background of the CSP represents the hills and mountains of the Council's high desert location. The steer and sheep indicate the region's extensive livestock ranching. The locomotive played a key part in the local history of gold and silver mining. Two old rail lines have been restored. One runs from Ruby Canyon to Great Basin National Park and the other from Virginia City to Gold Hill. The latter will soon be extended to Carson City, Nevada.
Scout_____ Date _____ Tel_____ E-mail _____

DANIEL WEBSTER Manchester, NH **Type** U **Issue** _____ **OA** Passaconaway #220
Description: This Council was named after the statesman, legislator, and orator, Daniel Webster. The state tree—the white birch; the state flower—the purple lilac shrub; and the state bird—the purple finch are all pictured. Also shown are the snow-covered White Mountains and Mt. Washington—the northeast's highest peak. Within these mountains are gaps, also known as "notches." The most famous is Franconia Notch, which creates a stone profile called the "Old Man of the Mountain." The lakes depicted are Winnipesaukee, Sunapee, and Winnisquam—the state's largest lake. The black line to the left forms the profile of a Boy Scout.
Scout_____ Date _____ Tel_____ E-mail _____

BURLINGTON COUNTY Rancocas, NJ **Type** N **Issue** '98 **OA** Hunnikick #76
Description: The bright red dragon emblazoned on this Council's CSP is the Jersey or Leeds Devil, part of the pineland area's folklore. The tale is the story of Mother Leeds of Burlington, N.J., a suspected witch, and her changeling son. When the son was born in 1735, he took the form of a dragon and terrorized the New Jersey countryside by eating little children and wreaking havoc. From time to time, the Jersey Devil is said to reappear. The last sighting was in 1899, except, of course, for the New Jersey Devils ice hockey team.
Scout_____ Date _____ Tel_____ E-mail _____

CENTRAL NEW JERSEY Monmouth Junction, NJ **Type** **Issue** '99 **OA** Sakuwit #2
Description: This Council was formed in 1999 by the merger of Thomas A. Edison and George Washington Councils. The name reflects the Council's location in the center of New Jersey. This understated patch features the outline of the state of New Jersey, with the golden star marking the Council's service area. Found within the Council's realm is Menlo Park, the site of the research laboratory where famous inventor Thomas Alva Edison (the "Wizard of Menlo Park") invented the incandescent light bulb. George Washington, the "Father of our Country" and the first President of the United States of America, fought and won the Battles of Princeton and Trenton in the Council's territory. These American Revolution battles were responsible for boosting American morale and leading the patriots on to victory.
Scout_____ Date _____ Tel_____ E-mail _____

New Jersey

N

N

JERSEY SHORE Toms River, NJ **Type** R **Issue** 9/92 **OA** Japeechen #341
Description: This CSP depicts the shoreline of New Jersey and one of its many sand dunes. The Council territory includes the shore communities of Long Beach, Seaside Heights, Beach Haven, and Atlantic City. These areas are well known for their beautiful beaches, boardwalks, amusement areas, resorts, and in the case of Atlantic City, casino gambling. The "Jersey Shore" is also a very popular boating and fishing area. Margate City features a very unusual attraction, Lucy the Elephant. This six story 90-ton building, in the shape of a pachyderm, is a National Historic Landmark offering tours, exhibits, and a gift shop.
Scout_____ Date _____ Tel_____ E-mail _____

MONMOUTH Oakhurst, NJ **Type** U **Issue** '72 **OA** Na-Tsi-Hi #71
Description: This patch is derived from the traditional patch design of the Council's Forestburg Scout Reservation. The design has been used since the camp opened in 1956. J. Fred Billett, the Council executive and camp director, designed the Forestburg patch. The Indian headdress represents the region's Native American history. The Revolutionary War skirmish, the Battle of Monmouth (June 28, 1778), took place in the Council's territory.
Scout_____ Date _____ Tel_____ E-mail _____

NORTHERN NEW JERSEY Fairlawn, NJ **Type** R **Issue** '99 **OA** Lenapehoking #IX
Description: This is the new name and patch for the former Bergen Council, which merged with Essex, Hudson Liberty, Passaic Valley, and Ridgewood-Glen Rock Councils in 1998. The simple design of this CSP features a map with the counties within New Jersey that make up the Council's service area. These counties are Bergen, Essex, Hudson, and Passaic. A fleur-de-lis is found superimposed on a compass rose. New Jersey was one of the original 13 colonies and the third to ratify the U.S. Constitution (1787).
Scout_____ Date _____ Tel_____ E-mail _____

PATRIOTS' PATH Mountainside, NJ **Type** N **Issue** '99 **OA** Allemakewink#54 Miquin#68
Description: This new Council was formed from the merger of Morris-Sussex and Watchung Councils. It covers Morris, Somerset, Sussex, and Union counties. A banner proudly hails the Council's new name. It was chosen via a contest and refers to the rich colonial history of the region. The use of red, white, and blue, as well as the cannon and flag represent the area's military fame. The Revolutionary Army spent four winters within the new Council's borders. Morristown was the headquarters for the army at least twice during the war. The army also made camp twice at Middlebrook, just north of Bound Brook. The Battle of Springfield also took place in the area. The historic "Victory Trail," runs from Elizabeth, N.J., to Springfield, N.J., and commemorates this battle. Pictured are two patriots marching down a Revolutionary War roadway. The patch also shows the so-called Betsy Ross flag, which was flown for the first time at the Battle of Springfield.
Scout_____ Date _____ Tel_____ E-mail _____

SOUTHERN NEW JERSEY Millville, NJ **Type** R **Issue** '99 **OA** Apatukwe #107
Description: This new CSP features the Delaware Memorial Bridge (Twin Bridge), which crosses the Delaware River and links the surrounding communities to the Council. Also pictured is the Cape May Lighthouse that is located on the southern most tip of New Jersey along the Atlantic Ocean. Its light shines on the Scouting fleur-de-lis, lighting the way for the Council's Scouts. The quaint Victorian-style city of Cape May is a popular tourist attraction. Another area site is Wheaton Village, an 88-acre re-creation of a glassmaking community of the late 1800's. Millville is one of the nation's largest glass-producing centers.
Scout_____ Date _____ Tel_____ E-mail _____

CONQUISTADOR Roswell, NM **Type** U **Issue** ____ **OA** Kwahadi #78
Description: The famous landscape artist and Scouter, Peter Hurd of San Patricio, N.M., designed this CSP. Mr. Hurd's paintings may be seen at the Roswell Museum and Art Center. This CSP features a Conquistador, a 16th century Spanish explorer. Superimposed in red, on the Conquistador, is the profile of a Boy Scout, a 20th century explorer. The ancient sun symbol of the Zia Pueblo Native Americans, on the left side of the patch, is the logo on New Mexico's state flag. The Council's home base, Roswell, was at the forefront of space exploration. From 1930 to 1945, Dr. Robert H. Goddard designed and tested rockets in his laboratory near Roswell, New Mexico.
Scout_____ Date _____ Tel_____ E-mail _____

GREAT SOUTHWEST Albuquerque, NM **Type** U **Issue** '95
                                                    OA Yah-Tah-Hey-Si-Kess #66
Description: The four state flags pictured represent each state the Council serves. From left to right they are: New Mexico, Colorado, Utah, and Arizona. The Council is home of Boy Scout's Philmont High Adventure Camp, located in Cimarron, New Mexico. Albuquerque's ideal wind and weather conditions make it a perfect location for hot air ballooning. Each October, Albuquerque plays host to the 9-day world acclaimed International Balloon Fiesta. The event features hundreds of hot air balloons of various shapes and designs. The city also features a number of museums and Old Town, the site of the city's original settlement.
Scout_____ Date _____ Tel_____ E-mail _____

ADIRONDACK Plattsburg, NY **Type** N **Issue** ____ **OA** Loon #364
Description: This unique CSP features the majestic Adirondack Mountains in purple, the blue waters of Lake Champlain, the clear blue sky, and the evergreen trees of the region's forests. The black and white border indicates the abundant white birch bark trees, which were an important resource for the local Native Americans. The Scouting symbol, the fleur-de-lis, is prominently featured in bright yellow.
Scout_____ Date _____ Tel_____ E-mail _____

V

ALLEGHENY HIGHLANDS Falconer, NY **Type** R **Issue** '73
OA Ho-Nan-Ne-Ho-Ont #165
Description: Incorporating areas in New York and Pennsylvania, this patch features a view of the beautiful terrain found in the Council area. Clear skies, the Allegheny River, the fertile green hills of the Allegheny State Forest, and the bright red-orange sun setting behind them are all common Council area sights. Places to visit include the Chautauqua Institution and the Kinzu Dam. The area is also host to the Lucille Ball Festival of New Comedy.
Scout_____ Date _____ Tel_____ E-mail _____

BADEN-POWELL Vestal, NY **Type** R **Issue** '98 **OA** Otahnagon #172
Description: Susquenango Council merged with Baden-Powell Council in January 1998. The three trees on this patch are from the old Susquenango CSP and represent this merger. They retained the Baden-Powell name, but took Susquenango's Council number, 368. The CSP honors Lord Baden-Powell, the founder of Boy Scouting. The blue background represents the Chenango and Susquehanna rivers, which were on the old Susquenango CSP, as well as Cayuga Lake where the former Baden-Powell's Camp Barton is located. Baden-Powell was an English war hero who wrote *Scouting for Boys*. In 1907, to test his theories, he took a group of boys on a camping trip. The successful experiment led Scout Patrols to spring up throughout England and the rest of the world. The rest is history.
Scout_____ Date _____ Tel_____ E-mail _____

CAYUGA COUNTY Auburn, NY **Type** R **Issue** _____ **OA** Tahgajute #247
Description: This CSP shows a Cayuga Native American paddling on one of the area's Finger Lakes, Lake Owasco. "Cayuga" means "The Place Where Locusts Were Taken Out." The Cayugas were one of the five original tribes that formed the Five Nations of the Iroquois. It wasn't until later that the Tuscarora tribe was added, making it the Six Nations of the Iroquois. During colonial times, Cayugas made their home in the Council's territory. In 1861, Auburn, N.Y., was an important stop along the Underground Railroad. The city contains the home of Harriet Tubman, a former slave who guided other slaves to freedom.
Scout_____ Date _____ Tel_____ E-mail _____

FINGER LAKES Geneva, NY **Type** U **Issue** '93 **OA** Ganeodiyo #417
Description: This Council is located in upstate New York. Their CSP features apple trees and a grapevine on the shores of one of the Finger Lakes. This region's climate is ideal for growing these fruits, and the apple orchards and vineyards contribute greatly to the local economy. According to Native American lore, God created the "Finger Lakes" by leaving his handprint on some of the most beautiful land ever created. There are eleven lakes that comprise the Finger Lakes. The larger ones are named for the tribes of the Six Nations of the Iroquois: Cayuga, Mohawk, Onondaga, Oneida, Seneca, and Tuscarora.
Scout_____ Date _____ Tel_____ E-mail _____

V, A   V

V, M   N

FIVE RIVERS Bath, NY **Type** U **Issue** '99 **OA** Tkäen Dõd #30
Description: This CSP is the same design, but with a stitching variation. Green fields and
rolling green hills create the perfect patch backdrop. The five flowing rivers shown are the
Chemung, Cohocton, Canisteo, Cowanesque, and Tioga. They merge together to form one
body of water. The name "Five Rivers" reflects the many regions included in this Council.
Scout_____ Date _____ Tel_____ E-mail _____
GENERAL HERKIMER Herkimer, NY **Type** U **Issue** '99 **OA** Kamargo #294
Description: This variation has a blue sky and black lettering. It depicts General Nicholas
Herkimer, though critically wounded, directing the successful Battle of Oriskany, a turning
point in the American Revolution. Much of the history of General Herkimer and the Coun-
cil's area is depicted in Walter Edmund's novel, *Drums Along The Mohawk*. A commem-
orative U.S. postage stamp was sponsored by the Council to raise funds for Scouting and to
commemorate the bicentennial of the battle. When in Herkimer, be sure to dig for the area's
"Herkimer Diamonds." These stones are rare, exceptionally clear quartz crystals.
Scout_____ Date _____ Tel_____ E-mail _____
GREATER NIAGARA FRONTIER Buffalo, NY **Type** N **Issue** '99
                                    OA Ho-De-No-Sau-Nee #159
Description: This new CSP is a slight design change. "New York" is at the bottom in brown.
It features a buffalo and waterfalls, denoting the consolidation of the Niagara Falls and Buf-
falo Councils. The falls also represent nature's unbridled power and grandeur, while the
white buffalo represents purity and strength of purpose, goals of the Scouting program. The
Council is located near the famous tourist spot, Niagara Falls, N.Y., location of the Ameri-
can Falls. The 184-foot high American Falls contains Bridal Veil Falls and the Cave of the
Winds. Visitors can enter the cave or take the Maid of the Mist boat ride to experience the
falls up close. Buffalo is also where hot and spicy "buffalo wings" were first served in 1964.
Scout_____ Date _____ Tel_____ E-mail _____
HIAWATHA-SEAWAY Syracuse, NY **Type** U **Issue** '99 **OA** Kayanernh -Kowa #219
Description: This new Council was formed from the merger of Hiawatha and Seaway Val-
ley Councils. The two councils are represented by the two canoeists. Hiawatha was a legendary Mohawk medicine man. He traveled through Iroquois country spreading the mes-
sage of unity and the Great Law of Peace. Hiawatha also helped form the Iroquois League
and was the inspiration for the long narrative poem, *The Song of Hiawatha,* by Henry
Wadsworth Longfellow. The St. Lawrence Seaway is home to the 6½-mile long Thousand
Islands International Bridge, which spans some of the islands that comprise the over 1,700
island group known as the Thousand Islands. The area serves as a gateway to the Thousand
Islands, the Adirondack Mountains resort area, and the St. Lawrence Islands National Park.
Scout_____ Date _____ Tel_____ E-mail _____

New York

GREATER NEW YORK New York, NY **Type** U **Issue** ____ **OA** Listed below
Description: The Greater New York Council is actually made up of five Councils from New
York City's five boroughs: Manhattan, Brooklyn, Staten Island, Queens, and the Bronx.
Two of these boroughs' patches feature the New York City skyline and the Statue of Liber-
ty. Staten Island's patch shows the Staten Island Ferry and the Verrazano-Narrows Bridge,
which link Staten Island with Manhattan and Brooklyn, respectively. Queens' patch shows
the Unisphere from the 1964 World's Fair, which took place in Flushing Meadows-Corona
Park. It also pictures flowers surrounded by a golden chain, representing the Queens Botan-
ical Gardens. The new 1998 Brooklyn patch features the world famous Brooklyn Bridge.
The bridge links Brooklyn with Manhattan. In addition, there is a "generic" patch for all the
New York City Councils. Although not pictured, the Council also produces special patches
bearing an Eagle for those Scouts who have attained the Eagle Rank.
OA Manhattan: Man-A-Hattin #82   **OA** Brooklyn: Shu-Shu-Gah #24
OA Staten Island: Aquehongian #112   **OA** Queens: Suanhacky #49
                     OA Bronx: Ranachqua #4

Scout_____ Date _____ Tel_____ E-mail _____
Scout_____ Date _____ Tel_____ E-mail _____
Scout_____ Date _____ Tel_____ E-mail _____
Scout_____ Date _____ Tel_____ E-mail _____
Scout_____ Date _____ Tel_____ E-mail _____
Scout_____ Date _____ Tel_____ E-mail _____

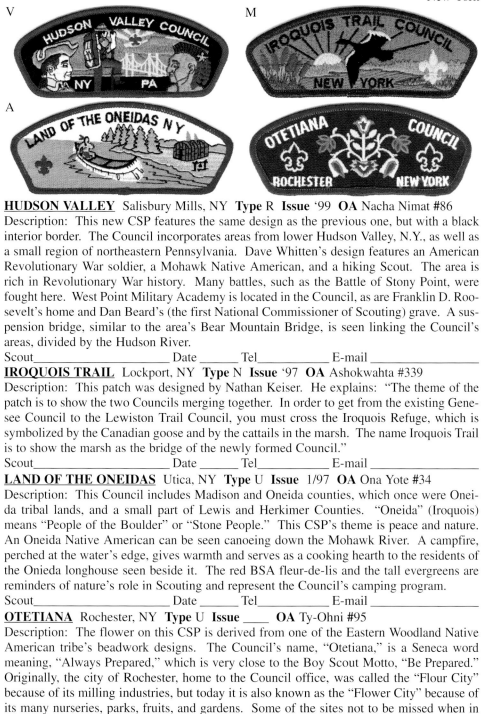

HUDSON VALLEY Salisbury Mills, NY **Type** R **Issue** '99 **OA** Nacha Nimat #86
Description: This new CSP features the same design as the previous one, but with a black interior border. The Council incorporates areas from lower Hudson Valley, N.Y., as well as a small region of northeastern Pennsylvania. Dave Whitten's design features an American Revolutionary War soldier, a Mohawk Native American, and a hiking Scout. The area is rich in Revolutionary War history. Many battles, such as the Battle of Stony Point, were fought here. West Point Military Academy is located in the Council, as are Franklin D. Roosevelt's home and Dan Beard's (the first National Commissioner of Scouting) grave. A suspension bridge, similar to the area's Bear Mountain Bridge, is seen linking the Council's areas, divided by the Hudson River.
Scout_____ Date _____ Tel_____ E-mail _____

IROQUOIS TRAIL Lockport, NY **Type** N **Issue** '97 **OA** Ashokwahta #339
Description: This patch was designed by Nathan Keiser. He explains: "The theme of the patch is to show the two Councils merging together. In order to get from the existing Genesee Council to the Lewiston Trail Council, you must cross the Iroquois Refuge, which is symbolized by the Canadian goose and by the cattails in the marsh. The name Iroquois Trail is to show the marsh as the bridge of the newly formed Council."
Scout_____ Date _____ Tel_____ E-mail _____

LAND OF THE ONEIDAS Utica, NY **Type** U **Issue** 1/97 **OA** Ona Yote #34
Description: This Council includes Madison and Oneida counties, which once were Oneida tribal lands, and a small part of Lewis and Herkimer Counties. "Oneida" (Iroquois) means "People of the Boulder" or "Stone People." This CSP's theme is peace and nature. An Oneida Native American can be seen canoeing down the Mohawk River. A campfire, perched at the water's edge, gives warmth and serves as a cooking hearth to the residents of the Onieda longhouse seen beside it. The red BSA fleur-de-lis and the tall evergreens are reminders of nature's role in Scouting and represent the Council's camping program.
Scout_____ Date _____ Tel_____ E-mail _____

OTETIANA Rochester, NY **Type** U **Issue** ____ **OA** Ty-Ohni #95
Description: The flower on this CSP is derived from one of the Eastern Woodland Native American tribe's beadwork designs. The Council's name, "Otetiana," is a Seneca word meaning, "Always Prepared," which is very close to the Boy Scout Motto, "Be Prepared." Originally, the city of Rochester, home to the Council office, was called the "Flour City" because of its milling industries, but today it is also known as the "Flower City" because of its many nurseries, parks, fruits, and gardens. Some of the sites not to be missed when in Rochester include the Strong Museum and the George Eastman House (Eastman Kodak Co.)—with its International Museum of Photography and Film.
Scout_____ Date _____ Tel_____ E-mail _____

New York

A

OTSCHODELA Oneonta, NY **Type** R **Issue** '79 **OA** Onteroraus #402
Description: The mountains represent the region between the Adirondack and Catskill Mountains. Oneonta is called "The City of the Hills." The home of the "Brotherhood of Railroad Workers" is represented by the caboose. An Indian is profiled, symbolizing the area's rich Native American history. The bat and ball signify that Cooperstown, the home of the Baseball Hall of Fame, is also in Council territory. The blue water stands for the area's many lakes and streams and the Susquehanna River. Howe Caverns are located here as well.
Scout_____ Date _____ Tel_____ E-mail _____

RIP VAN WINKLE Kingston, NY **Type** N **Issue** '94 **OA** Half Moon #28
Description: This Council is named for the well known short story written by Washington Irving, "Rip Van Winkle" (1820). In the story, Rip Van Winkle and his dog, Wolf, fall asleep in the Catskill Mountains for 20 years. They awake to find a completely new society. Rip and Wolf are pictured sleeping on the CSP. In the background are the three mountains in the Catskill range for which the Council's Camp Tri Mount is named. In 1777, the city of Kingston was the first capital of New York State. The house where the state senate met is open to the public as a museum.
Scout_____ Date _____ Tel_____ E-mail _____

SUFFOLK COUNTY Medford, NY **Type** U **Issue** ____ **OA** Shinnecock #360
Description: An outline of Suffolk County, New York, is pictured with the ocean, whales, and sea gulls that are found in the area. The county and Council are located on the eastern end of Long Island, which is divided into the North and South Forks. Southampton, a famous summer seaside resort area for the rich and famous, is found on the South Fork. Southhampton is also home to the Shinnecock Indian Reservation. Deep-sea fishing and oystering are important industries and pastimes in Suffolk.
Scout_____ Date _____ Tel_____ E-mail _____

THEODORE ROOSEVELT Massapequa, NY **Type** U **Issue** '97 **OA** Buckskin #412
Description: Formerly Nassau County Council, this new name honors the Council's First Commissioner, President Theodore Roosevelt. The CSP, designed by Michael Luzzi, Troop 369, Valley Stream, New York, features Roosevelt's likeness. For many years the Council's Scouts would make a pilgrimage to Theodore Roosevelt's home, "Sagamore Hills," in Oyster Bay, Long Island. The golden Scouting fleur-de-lis is pictured amid the landscape of Nassau County. The tent highlights the Council's camping program. Nassau County's north shore is known as the "Gold Coast" due to its many lavish estates, beautiful gardens, and fine shops. On the south shore are Jones Beach—a popular summer retreat, and the Atlantic Ocean.
Scout_____ Date _____ Tel_____ E-mail _____

B

M

TWIN RIVERS Albany, NY **Type** U **Issue** 1992 **OA** Ganienkeh #19
Description: The canoe symbolizes the area's rich Native American history. The tree represents the region's many forests, and the fire signifies the camping spirit of Boy Scouting. The Mohawk and Hudson Rivers flow through Council territory, giving the Council its name. Of special interest in the area are Saratoga Battlefield National Park—home to a Scout Historic Trail; the United States Arsenal; Lake George Battleground Park; and Fort Ticondergoa. Albany, the state capital of New York, is home to the Empire State Plaza—site of the New York State Government and State Museum. This patch was designed by A. J. Siatkowski. Mohican Council merged with Twin Rivers Council on August 31, 1998.
Scout_____ Date _____ Tel_____ E-mail _____

WESTCHESTER-PUTNAM Hawthorne, NY **Type** R **Issue** '99 **OA** Ktemaque #15
Description: This Council's CSP has returned to the one used before its 25th anniversary patch. The Council was originally called Washington Irving Council, in honor of the famous author, but changed its name to Westchester-Putnam after merging with the Hutchinson River Council. The bridge on this CSP symbolizes the Tappan Zee Bridge, as well as the "haunted" bridge from Washington Irving's short story, "The Legend of Sleepy Hollow." The Headless Horseman from the story is seen riding over the Headless Horseman Bridge which is located in Sleepy Hollow, New York (formerly North Tarrytown). Sunnyside, the country home of Washington Irving, is a local museum.
Scout_____ Date _____ Tel_____ E-mail _____

CAPE FEAR Wilmington, NC **Type** U **Issue** '85 **OA** Klahican #331
Description: The lighthouse on this CSP symbolizes the lighthouse found on Bald Head Island. It also represents the other beacons placed along the inlet to guide ships navigating the Cape Fear River. This Council is located in Wilmington, N.C., the main deepwater port on the Cape Fear River. The city was the colonial capital in 1743 and the site of the Stamp Act Rebellion of 1765. Area sites include the Battleship North Carolina, the Cape Fear Museum, Poplar Grove Historic Plantation, and the Wilmington Railroad Museum.
Scout_____ Date _____ Tel_____ E-mail _____

CENTRAL NORTH CAROLINA Albermarle, NC **Type** U **Issue** '68
OA Iti Bapishe Iti Hollo #188
Description: This CSP shows the shape of the state of North Carolina in green with the Council area in yellow. Also included is the North Carolina state flag. The structure with the cross is the Council's camp chapel, a reminder of a Scout's duty to God. The fleur-de-lis with the American bald eagle centered in it, the symbol of Boy Scouting, is pictured as well. Within the Council's territory, rockhounds can pan for gold at the Cottonpatch Gold Mine, or visitors can enjoy a trip to Morrow Mountain State Park.
Scout_____ Date _____ Tel_____ E-mail _____

DANIEL BOONE Asheville, NC **Type** U **Issue** _____ **OA** Tsali #134
Description: This Council is named in honor of the famous American frontiersman, Daniel Boone. Pictured are the Blue Ridge Mountains and the Kentucky Long Rifle, the type of musket used by Boone. In the 1760's, Daniel Boone had a cabin in the Council's area. The Council's office is located in Asheville, a noted resort area located on a high plateau between the Blue Ridge and Great Smoky Mountains. Asheville is the headquarter city of the Blue Ridge Mountain Parkway and gateway to the Cherokee Indian Reservation. It is the boyhood home of author Thomas Clayton Wolfe, writer of _Look Homeward, Angel_ (1929).
Scout_____ Date _____ Tel_____ E-mail _____

EAST CAROLINA Kinston, NC **Type** U **Issue** 8/93 **OA** Croatan #117
Description: The deer and blue heron depicted are abundantly found in the East Carolina service area. Also included are Cape Lookout Lighthouse, the Atlantic Ocean, the sun, sea gulls, and the Scout fleur-de-lis. The area is well known as a mecca for bluegrass music lovers. Kinston is home to the Eastern North Carolina Bluegrass Association, a group dedicated to increasing the public awareness of bluegrass and its heritage. When the city of Kinston was originally founded in 1762, it was called Kingston. The "g" was later dropped, by Revolutionary Patriots, to disassociate the city from England and the king.
Scout_____ Date _____ Tel_____ E-mail _____

MECKLENBURG COUNTY Charlotte, NC **Type** R **Issue** _____ **OA** Catawba #459
Description: Pictured is an area icon—the hornet's nest with three small hornets, which relates to a statement made by the British General, Charles Cornwallis, during the American Revolution. He referred to Charlotte as a "Hornet's Nest of Rebellion." It also represents the Council's "beehive" of activities, and the hornet's nest is the OA totem. The musket symbolizes the area's involvement in the American Revolution and the Civil War. In April 1865, during the Civil War, Jefferson Davis, President of the Confederacy, convened his full Cabinet here for the last time. The spear represents the area's Native American heritage. The Catawbas, "People of the River," inhabited the border region between the Carolinas. The golden crown represents Charlotte's nickname, "The Queen City," so named for Queen Charlotte Sophia of Mecklenburg-Strelitz, wife of King George III of Great Britain.
Scout_____ Date _____ Tel_____ E-mail _____

OCCONEECHEE Raleigh, NC **Type** U **Issue** _____ **OA** Occoneechee #104
Description: This CSP exemplifies the beauty of this Council's territory. On the left are North Carolina's state bird—the cardinal, and the state flower—the flowering dogwood. The center depicts the Council's area within North Carolina. The squirrel symbolizes the area's indigenous wildlife. The sun is shines over the land. Raleigh, the state capital, was named for explorer Sir Walter Raleigh. Raleigh is the birthplace of President Andrew Johnson.
Scout_____ Date _____ Tel_____ E-mail _____

A

M

OLD HICKORY Winston-Salem, NC **Type** R **Issue** '82 **OA** Wahissa #118
Description: This CSP depicts a midnight view across Lake Sabotta at Raven Knob Scout Reservation. As the moon rises, it shimmers over the lake, where the silhouette of the totem pole can be seen. The outline of Raven Knob Mountain is in the background, while the shadows of hickory trees are in the foreground. The Council is named for Andrew "Old Hickory" Jackson. He operated his first law practice within the areas now served by the Old Hickory Council. The Council is located in Winston-Salem. The "Winston" part of the city name comes from Major Joseph Winston, a Revolutionary War hero. The "Salem" was derived from "shalom," the Hebrew word for "peace."
Scout_____ Date _____ Tel_____ E-mail _____

OLD NORTH STATE Greensboro, NC **Type** U **Issue** 5/95 **OA** Tsoiotsi Tsogalii #70
Description: This patch is a replica of the flag of North Carolina. This Council's name is a reference to North Carolina's nickname, the "Old North State." The area was the home of famous short story writer William Sydney Porter, better known as O. Henry. It was also the home of the fourth U.S. First Lady, Dolley Madison, and journalist Edward R. Morrow.
Scout_____ Date _____ Tel_____ E-mail _____

PIEDMONT Gastonia, NC **Type** R **Issue** ____ **OA** Eswau Huppeday #560
Description: This CSP depicts the eleven counties that this Council serves (shown in black within the map of North Carolina) and uses the colors found in its state flag. "Piedmont" refers to one of three regions that make up North Carolina. The Piedmont, which is an area at the foot of a mountain or mountain range, starts at the base of the Blue Ridge Mountain chain and covers about half the state. One of the Council area's tourist attractions is The Schiele Museum of Natural History and Planetarium. The area is known as a large textile-manufacturing region. Each October, the city of Gastonia celebrates Textile Week.
Scout_____ Date _____ Tel_____ E-mail _____

TUSCARORA Goldsboro, NC **Type** U **Issue** ____ **OA** Nayawin Rar #296
Description: This Council was named after the Iroquoian speaking tribe that originally lived in the area, especially along the Roanoke, Tar, Pamlico, and Neuse Rivers, near Cape Hatteras. A likeness of a Tuscarora Native American is seen on the patch. In the early 1760's, the tribe migrated to New York State where they later became the Sixth Nation of the Iroquois League. The American flag reminds us that the Battle of Bentonville, a Union victory and one of the last major engagements of the American Civil War, was fought nearby (March 1865). The flag also represents the Scout's loyalty to his country. The words "for God and Country," part of the Boy Scout Oath, are found on the banner, emphasizing this commitment to loyalty and expanding it to include devotion to God.
Scout_____ Date _____ Tel_____ E-mail _____

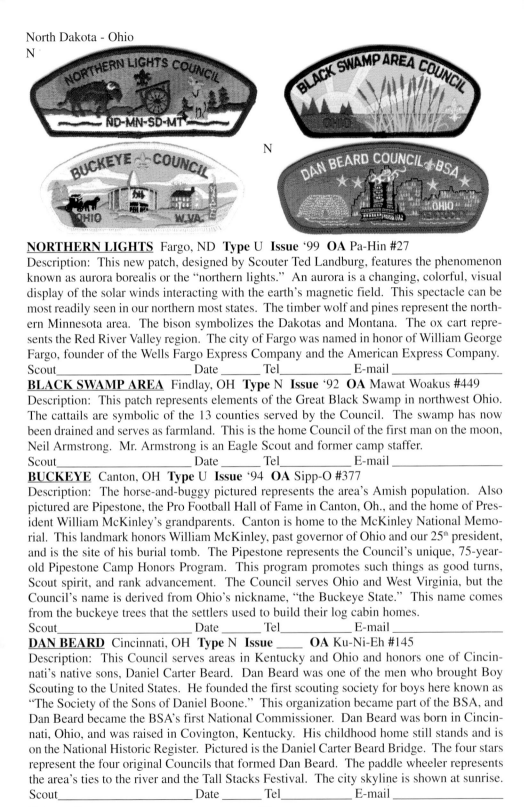

N

NORTHERN LIGHTS Fargo, ND **Type** U **Issue** '99 **OA** Pa-Hin #27
Description: This new patch, designed by Scouter Ted Landburg, features the phenomenon known as aurora borealis or the "northern lights." An aurora is a changing, colorful, visual display of the solar winds interacting with the earth's magnetic field. This spectacle can be most readily seen in our northern most states. The timber wolf and pines represent the northern Minnesota area. The bison symbolizes the Dakotas and Montana. The ox cart represents the Red River Valley region. The city of Fargo was named in honor of William George Fargo, founder of the Wells Fargo Express Company and the American Express Company.
Scout_____ Date _____ Tel_____ E-mail _____

BLACK SWAMP AREA Findlay, OH **Type** N **Issue** '92 **OA** Mawat Woakus #449
Description: This patch represents elements of the Great Black Swamp in northwest Ohio. The cattails are symbolic of the 13 counties served by the Council. The swamp has now been drained and serves as farmland. This is the home Council of the first man on the moon, Neil Armstrong. Mr. Armstrong is an Eagle Scout and former camp staffer.
Scout_____ Date _____ Tel_____ E-mail _____

BUCKEYE Canton, OH **Type** U **Issue** '94 **OA** Sipp-O #377
Description: The horse-and-buggy pictured represents the area's Amish population. Also pictured are Pipestone, the Pro Football Hall of Fame in Canton, Oh., and the home of President William McKinley's grandparents. Canton is home to the McKinley National Memorial. This landmark honors William McKinley, past governor of Ohio and our 25th president, and is the site of his burial tomb. The Pipestone represents the Council's unique, 75-year-old Pipestone Camp Honors Program. This program promotes such things as good turns, Scout spirit, and rank advancement. The Council serves Ohio and West Virginia, but the Council's name is derived from Ohio's nickname, "the Buckeye State." This name comes from the buckeye trees that the settlers used to build their log cabin homes.
Scout_____ Date _____ Tel_____ E-mail _____

DAN BEARD Cincinnati, OH **Type** N **Issue** _____ **OA** Ku-Ni-Eh #145
Description: This Council serves areas in Kentucky and Ohio and honors one of Cincinnati's native sons, Daniel Carter Beard. Dan Beard was one of the men who brought Boy Scouting to the United States. He founded the first scouting society for boys here known as "The Society of the Sons of Daniel Boone." This organization became part of the BSA, and Dan Beard became the BSA's first National Commissioner. Dan Beard was born in Cincinnati, Ohio, and was raised in Covington, Kentucky. His childhood home still stands and is on the National Historic Register. Pictured is the Daniel Carter Beard Bridge. The four stars represent the four original Councils that formed Dan Beard. The paddle wheeler represents the area's ties to the river and the Tall Stacks Festival. The city skyline is shown at sunrise.
Scout_____ Date _____ Tel_____ E-mail _____

N  M

A

ERIE SHORES Toledo, OH **Type** U **Issue** '99 **OA** Tindeuchen #522
Description: This is the new name for the former Toledo Area Council. The Council's new CSP features the lighthouse found on Catawba Island. Lake Erie is the southern most and shallowest Great Lake. The lake's depth (62-feet on average) makes travel difficult during storms, requiring the use of lighthouses such as the one on this patch. On the patch's right is a representation of Toledo, Ohio's downtown area. The freighter, behind the skyscrapers, represents the city's place as one of the world's busiest freshwater ports. The farm scene, on the left, symbolizes the region's many small farms. Corn and soybeans are the two main crops of the state. The sailboat represents the numerous watersports available on the lake.
Scout_____ Date _____ Tel_____ E-mail _____
GREAT TRAIL Akron, OH **Type** U **Issue** ____ **OA** Marnoc #151
Description: This CSP features the gateway to the Council's camp, Camp Manatoc, founded in 1931. The camp is located in Cuyahoga Valley National Recreation Area. Akron is called the "Rubber Capital of the World" due to the area's large production of tires by the B.F. Goodrich Tire Company. It is also the home of the All-American Soap Box Derby, the World Series of Golf, and bowling's Tournament of Champions.
Scout_____ Date _____ Tel_____ E-mail _____
GREATER CLEVELAND Cleveland, OH **Type** U **Issue** ____ **OA** Cuyahoga #17
Description: This CSP features Cleveland's skyline. The major downtown area is divided into three sections: the Mall, which includes the county, city, and federal buildings, the public library, and the convention center; the Public Square, an area of civic monuments, containing Ohio's tallest building—the 948-foot Society Center, and the recently renovated Tower City Center; and Erieview Plaza, an urban redevelopment project. Also shown are the region's suburban homes. The city is home to The Rock-and-Roll Hall of Fame.
Scout_____ Date _____ Tel_____ E-mail _____
GREATER WESTERN RESERVE Painesville, OH **Type** U **Issue** 5/96
OA Wapashuwi #56
Description: This patch (designer Star Scout Keith Antosh) tells the story of the Great Council Chief who instructed a young brave to call all Scouts who live in the six counties (represented by the six hills) to come together in brotherhood. From Lake Erie, the wooded hills, and the grassy fields, three small Councils joined to become one. They strive to make this Council better than any of the previous Councils. We are reminded to reach for the stars by the full moon and clear sky. The Scout emblem, like a compass, always points to the right way in life. In northeast Ohio, we see the Council fire rising from the cabin, as the moon rises from the horizon. Symbolic of brotherhood, the fire warms the Scout and guides his way through the darkness.
Scout_____ Date _____ Tel_____ E-mail _____

Ohio

B, M

HEART OF OHIO Mansfield, OH **Type** N **Issue** 12/98 **OA** Portage #619
Description: This patch was designed by Ed Hindel, a leader from Cub Scout Pack 246 in East Townsend. Mr. Hindel had this to say about the CSP's symbolism: "The Heart of Ohio Council is surrounded by rolling farmland, wooded areas, and Lake Erie Shoreland." The Council's placement within the state of Ohio is marked in red. The lighthouse is a generic one and represents Lake Erie. The Council is at the heart of the nine county area it serves.
Scout_____ Date _____ Tel_____ E-mail _____

MIAMI VALLEY Dayton, OH **Type** U **Issue** ____ **OA** Miami #495
Description: This Council is located in the region known as Miami Valley. The name is derived from the Miami Native Americans, who inhabited the area. Miami (Algonquian) means "People of the Peninsula." The biplane denotes that Dayton was the home of Wilbur and Orville Wright. The brothers did their pioneering research on aircraft here. Dayton, known as the "Birthplace of Aviation," is still at the forefront of aerospace and high-technology. Located in the city are the various sites of the Dayton Aviation Heritage National Historical Park where you can explore the Wright Brothers' bicycle shop and see the airfield where they tested one of their early plane designs. Dayton was also the birthplace of poet and novelist Paul Laurence Dunbar (1872). He was one of the first black writers to gain national distinction. The cricket pictured on the patch was designed for the Council by the famous cartoonist, Milton Caniff. It represents Cricket Hollow, the Council's camp.
Scout_____ Date _____ Tel_____ E-mail _____

MUSKINGUM VALLEY Zanesville, OH **Type** U **Issue** '98 **OA** Netawatwees #424
Description: This CSP is a return to the pre-John Glenn patch. It was designed to highlight the Ohio state bird—the cardinal; the state tree—the Ohio buckeye; and the state flag. The blue shape of Ohio is in the center of the CSP, with the yellow representing the four counties that make up this Council's territory. The colors used also represent the types of Scouting: blue and gold—Cub Scouting; red and gold—Boy Scouting; and green and brown—Explorers. The Council's area contains the boyhood home of astronaut and senator, John Glenn.
Scout_____ Date _____ Tel_____ E-mail _____

SIMON KENTON Columbus, OH **Type** N **Issue** 5/95 **OA** Tecumseh #65
Description: Simon Kenton is paddling his canoe on this patch. Kenton was a great scout, Indian fighter, and frontiersman, who, along with Daniel Boone, helped to settle the Ohio and Kentucky areas. Columbus, where the Council office is located, is the capital of Ohio and its largest city. The Columbus area is a demographically normal cross section of America and is renowned for technological advances. The city is often used in the testing of new fast food menus and other products, earning it the nickname, "Test Market, USA."
Scout_____ Date _____ Tel_____ E-mail _____

TECUMSEH Springfield, OH **Type** N **Issue** ____ **OA** Tarhe #292
Description: This Council is named in honor of Ohio's great Shawnee chief, Tecumseh. The CSP features his likeness. Tecumseh opposed surrendering Native American lands to whites. He believed it was illegal for any one tribe to do so without the consent of all the others. He and his brother, Tenskwatawa, warned other Native Americans against adopting the white man's way of life. In addition to Tecumseh, pictured on this CSP are sites found at Camp Hugh Taylor Birch: the rappelling tower, Morris "Bud" Martin Lake, and Carmony Lodge—the oldest cabin at the camp. E.J. Carmony built this log cabin in 1936. The bird is a crane, the OA mascot, and the skunk is affectionately known as a "Birch Cat."
Scout_____ Date _____ Tel_____ E-mail _____

ARBUCKLE AREA Ardmore, OK **Type** N **Issue** ____ **OA** Wisawanik #190
Description: This Council was named for the Arbuckle Mountains, which straddle the region and are drawn on this patch. Within the Arbuckle Mountains are the scenic Turner Falls, pictured on the CSP's left. "Oklahoma," a Muskogean word, coined by Choctaw Allen Wright, means "Red People." In 1890, part of the state was set aside as a settlement for Native Americans and was known as the "Indian Territory." Oklahoma's Native American heritage is reflected by the Oklahoma Shield, which is found on the state flag, the state license plate, and on this CSP.
Scout_____ Date _____ Tel_____ E-mail _____

CHEROKEE AREA Bartlesville, OK **Type** U **Issue** '72 **OA** Washita #288
Description: This patch pictures the Bartlesville, Ok., oil well that was the first productive commercial well in Oklahoma. The American bison on this CSP represents the thousands of bison that once roamed the area. Bison were very important to the Native Americans who used them for food, clothing, tools, and fuel. The Indian chief's head, centered on the patch, symbolizes the region's many Native American tribes.
Scout_____ Date _____ Tel_____ E-mail _____

GREAT SALT PLAINS Enid, OK **Type** U **Issue** ____ **OA** Ah-Ska #213
Description: This Council patch is embroidered on a white (salt) background and features the American flag. The bald eagle, with bundles of wheat in its beak, represents Salt Plains National Wildlife Refuge and the area's plentiful wheat. The Salt Plains, which are covered by a thin layer of salt, were once greatly valued. Today, many visitors still come to the salt flats to mine for selenite crystals. The region's salt flats are among the largest in the midwest. The Council is headquartered in Enid, Oklahoma. It is said the town's name came from Alfred Lord Tennyson's poem, "Idylls of the King," but rumor has it that the name actually came from cattle drivers who turned the "DINE" sign on a cook's tent up-side down.
Scout_____ Date _____ Tel_____ E-mail _____

INDIAN NATIONS Tulsa, OK **Type** U **Issue** '85 **OA** Ta Tsu Hwa #138
Description: The blue background on this CSP is the same color as the Oklahoma state flag. Oklahoma is shown in red with a tepee and headdress to symbolize the area's Native American heritage. The Council territory is comprised of the Five Civilized Tribes of the Indian Territory (Cherokee, Chickasaw, Choctaw, Creek, and Seminole). According to the 1990 census, Oklahoma has the third largest Native American population in the United States.
Scout_____ Date _____ Tel_____ E-mail _____

LAST FRONTIER Oklahoma City, OK **Type** N **Issue** '92 **OA** Ma-Nu #133
Description: The three tepees represent the area's "Indian Territory" heritage. Members of 39 Native American Tribes are found throughout Oklahoma. Oil wells are familiar sights within the city limits and are responsible for the area's economy. More than 2,000 wells are found in the city and surrounding areas. The region's most famous oil strike was the Mary Sudik (1930). It lasted 11 days and spread oil for 15 miles. This area of Oklahoma was the last to be settled, thus the Council's name. On April 22, 1889, from noon until sundown, the unsettled prairie lands of the Oklahoma Territory (land that was not set aside as Indian Territory) were opened for settlement; more than 10,000 claims were made that afternoon. Oklahoma City, literally, sprung up overnight. The space shuttle, planets, and stars are icons representing the future of this region and Scouting. They also symbolize the area's aviation industry. Black Beaver Council merged into Last Frontier in 1996.
Scout_____ Date _____ Tel_____ E-mail _____

WILL ROGERS Ponca City, OK **Type** R **Issue** ____ **OA** Inola #148
Description: The image of Oklahoma, with a Native American bird design, is a reminder of the state's importance as a home to large numbers of Native Americans from many different tribes. The Council name honors the great American humorist, actor, and writer Will Rogers. William Penn Adair Rogers was born (1879) and is buried (1935) in the small town of Oologah (near Claremore, Oklahoma). Rogers was famous for his political wit and for his rope tricks. His burial site is in Indian Territory, within the Council's service area.
Scout_____ Date _____ Tel_____ E-mail _____

CASCADE PACIFIC Portland, OR **Type** U **Issue** 1/94 **OA** Wauna La-Mon'Tay #442
Description: Pictured on this patch is Mt. Hood (the tallest mountain in Oregon at 11,239-feet) in the Oregon Cascade. It is about 50 miles from Portland, home to the Council's office. Portland, Oregon's largest city, was named in 1845 by city co-founder, Francis Pettygrove, who won naming rights via a coin toss (If he had lost, the city would have been named Boston). The city was originally called "Stumptown" due to the numerous tree stumps that stood in the city. The blue water represents the Pacific Ocean. The salmon and forest symbolize Oregon's natural resources.
Scout_____ Date _____ Tel_____ E-mail _____

N, M

N, M, A

CRATER LAKE Central Point, OR **Type** U **Issue** '96 **OA** Lo La 'Qam Geela #491
Description: This CSP was designed by a Council Scout as part of a Council CSP design contest. The patch features the island, "Phantom Ship," in Crater Lake, so named because it resembles a ship under sail. The deep blue represents the water of Crater Lake, known for its intense color, which is a result of the clarity and depth of the lake. It is the second deepest lake in North America and occupies the crater of the prehistoric volcano, Mount Mazama. Also on the patch is an American bald eagle. The city of Central Point is so named because it was at the intersection of two stagecoach routes.
Scout_____ Date _____ Tel_____ E-mail _____

OREGON TRAIL Eugene, OR **Type** U **Issue** '99 **OA** Tsisqan #253
Description: This new patch design features pioneers in a covered wagon traveling the Oregon Trail. The trail was an overland pioneer route running from the Columbia River in Oregon to Independence, Missouri. A spectacular waterfall graces the patch's background and represents the region's many falls. A bald eagle soars over the Douglas Fir (the state tree) covered mountains. Oregon is noted for its fine lumber and supplies the nation with most of its softwood plywood. More commercial timber comes from here than any other state, except Alaska. Willamette National Forest is found in this Council's territory. The Council's service area extends from the top of the Cascade Mountains to the Oregon coast.
Scout_____ Date _____ Tel_____ E-mail _____

BUCKS COUNTY Doylestown, PA **Type** U **Issue** '99 **OA** Ajapeu #33
Description: This new CSP features the same basic design, but the border is red and "90th Anniversary B.S.A." is written across the top. The Council is located just north of Philadelphia. It was here that George Washington crossed the Delaware River. The silver scene on this CSP depicts this event. This scene was taken from the famous 1871 painting by Emanuel Lutze, which hangs in the Metropolitan Museum of Art in New York City. The first U.S. flag, purportedly designed by Betsy Ross, serves as the patch's background.
Scout_____ Date _____ Tel_____ E-mail _____

BUCKTAIL Du Bois, PA **Type** U **Issue** ____ **OA** Ah-tic #139
Description: This CSP shows west central Pennsylvania's terrain with its mountains, pine trees, water, and wildlife, including bucktail deer. The Council acquired its name from the "Bucktail Regiment" that fought here during the Civil War era, and still issues "bucktails" to its members who attend national events. The region contains the only herd of elk east of the Rockies. The area is home to world famous groundhog, Punxsutawney Phil. Each February 2nd, since 1887, the groundhog predicts whether or not there will be an early spring. If he sees his shadow, we are in for another six weeks of winter. When in town, be sure to visit Mahoning East Civic Center where there is a life-size statue of Phil and a groundhog zoo.
Scout_____ Date _____ Tel_____ E-mail _____

Pennsylvania

CHESTER COUNTY West Chester, PA **Type** N **Issue** '95 **OA** Octoraro #22
Description: The covered bridge shown on this patch is one of seventeen in the county and
crosses Octoraro Creek. The bridge, along with the monkey bridge near the tree, also represents the bridging of two counties: Chester County, Pennsylvania, and northeastern Cecil
County, Maryland. The sun shines on all Scouting families within these two areas, joined
as one under Chester County Council. As well as portraying the "sun," the hunt horn symbolizes that the area is one of the last vestiges of foxhunts in the country.
Scout_____ Date _____ Tel_____ E-mail _____

CHIEF CORNPLANTER Warren, PA **Type** U **Issue** '84 **OA** Gyantwachia #255
Description: Pictured on the left is Chief Cornplanter, a famous Seneca chief, trusted by
both Indians and settlers. Chief Cornplanter worked to arrange several treaties that brought
peace to the frontier. Also pictured is the Kinzua Dam, built in the early 1960's, on the
Allegheny River. This dam controls flooding in communities from Warren to Pittsburgh.
The dam created the Kinzua Reservoir, a vast recreational area. Pictured in the background
are the Allegheny Mountains. All this is located in the Allegheny National Forest, a haven
for boating, camping, climbing, fishing, hiking, and hunting. The Council's Camp Olmsted
is located on the banks of the Kinzua Reservoir.
Scout_____ Date _____ Tel_____ E-mail _____

COLUMBIA-MONTOUR Bloomsburg, PA **Type** R **Issue** 7/95 **OA** Wyona #18
Description: This patch, designed by Mark Jones, incorporates the natural features of the
area and things of significance to the Columbia and Montour County regions. Pictured on
the CSP are rolling hills, the Susquehanna River, farmland, covered bridges, and an elk. An
elk has been used on the Council's patches since their first patch design, 75 years ago. It is
also the OA totem.
Scout_____ Date _____ Tel_____ E-mail _____

CRADLE OF LIBERTY Philadelphia, PA **Type** N **Issue** ____ **OA** Unami #1
Description: This Council was formerly the Philadelphia and Valley Forge Councils. Pennsylvania, second to join the Union, played a pivotal role in the creation of the United States.
Pictured is Independence Hall. It served as the meeting place of the Continental Congress
(1775-1781) and as the birthplace of both the Declaration of Independence (July 4, 1776)
and the United States Constitution (1787). It was also home to the U.S. Supreme Court
(1789-1800). Independence Hall and the Liberty Bell form part of Independence National
Historical Park. Also in the Council is Valley Forge National Historical Park, the site where
American Revolutionary War leader George Washington kept his winter headquarters.
Annual Scout encampments have been held here since 1911. The flag of the original 13
states is also pictured.
Scout_____ Date _____ Tel_____ E-mail _____

FRENCH CREEK Erie, PA **Type** N **Issue** '99 **OA** Langundowi #46
Description: The new French Creek CSP design replaces one that had been in use for almost 30 years. Its unique diamond-shape was due to an error made by the embroidery company. The CSP features an American bison (buffalo) overlooking French Creek at the joining of Deer Creek. The buffalo appears as a reference to the French, who were the first to explore and fortify the area and called French Creek "Rivierre Le Beouf" or "Buffalo River." The waterway, which is in fact a river, was misnamed "French Creek" by George Washington. It flows through the entire length of the Council's boundaries. The three fleur-de-lis are not the BSA icons, but are of the French style and are of the same type as those found on the former French Royal Standard flag that was in use prior to the French and Indian War. Also displayed are fallen logs, other common area flora, and one of the region's colorful sunsets. The rustic looking Celtic-hand font and its placement, along with the lack of other words, were specifically designed not to distract from the overall beauty of the patch.
Scout_____ Date _____ Tel_____ E-mail _____

GREATER PITTSBURGH Pittsburgh, PA **Type** U **Issue** ____ **OA** Enda Lechauhanne #57
Description: This CSP depicts the "Renaissance" of Pittsburgh from the "Smoky City" (due to the smoke that spewed from the stacks used by the early, unregulated steel industry) to the city of today. Pittsburgh's downtown business area, "The Golden Triangle," and the Pittsburgh State Park Fountain are shown. The water represents the confluence of the Allegheny, Monongahela, and Ohio Rivers. Many battles between the British and French to control the Ohio Valley were fought on these rivers. On the left is Fort Duquesne Bridge, and on the right, Fort Pitt Bridge. Pittsburgh, the "City of Bridges," has 720 bridges.
Scout_____ Date _____ Tel_____ E-mail _____

HAWK MOUNTAIN Reading, PA **Type** U **Issue** '76 **OA** Kittatinny #5
Description: This patch proudly displays our country's colors and features "Herbie Hawk," the Council's mascot. The Council's name comes from the area's Hawk Mountain Bird Sanctuary. Area attractions include American frontiersman Daniel Boone's birthplace—the Daniel Boone Homestead; the Boyertown Museum of Historic Vehicles; a coal mine tour; and the Pagoda—a seven-story 1908 Japanese-style building with a city view.
Scout_____ Date _____ Tel_____ E-mail _____

JUNIATA VALLEY Reedsville, PA **Type** U **Issue** '86 **OA** Monaken #103
Description: This CSP was designed by members of the Monaken OA Lodge. The patch depicts the Juniata River flowing through mountains. Shown are the area's evergreens, and the rising sun can be seen behind the Seven Mountains (home to the Council's Scout camp). The Council is home to Lincoln Caverns and Penns Cave. The Council area also lays claim to Raystown Lake, the largest lake entirely located in Pennsylvania.
Scout_____ Date _____ Tel_____ E-mail _____

Pennsylvania
V
M
B

KEYSTONE AREA Mechanicsburg, PA **Type** R **Issue** '99 **OA** Susquehannock #11
Description: This patch is a variation on the old one, but the lettering and keystone have been made smaller. This Council takes its name from Pennsylvania's nickname, "the Keystone State." This nickname refers to both the state's political importance and its location as the middle state of the 13 original states. This CSP expresses the Council's state patriotism and proud heritage by featuring mountain laurel (state flower), a ruffed grouse (state bird), and the State Capitol Building in Harrisburg, Pennsylvania. Harrisburg, within the Council's territory, became the State Capital in 1812. The Capitol Building, built in 1906, features a dome modeled after the one on Saint Peter's Basilica in Rome, Italy.
Scout_____ Date _____ Tel_____ E-mail _____

MINSI TRAILS Lehigh Valley, PA **Type** U **Issue** '69 **OA** Witauchsoman #44
Description: The trees on this patch represent the thirteen districts of the original three Councils that merged to form Minsi Trails. The doves symbolize the peaceful merger of the Lehigh, Bethlehem Area, and Delaware Valley Area Councils. The white area represents the Scouting "Trails." The name "Minsi" was selected because is was significant to all three Councils. Area visitors may enjoy the charm of Bethlehem's 18th Century Moravian community and thrill to a day at Downy Park and Wildwater Kingdom. During the American Revolution, the Liberty Bell was hidden at Zion's Reformed Church in Allentown, Pennsylvania (1777). The British had taken over Philadelphia, and it was feared they would capture the bell, a famous symbol of freedom.
Scout_____ Date _____ Tel_____ E-mail _____

MORAINE TRAILS Butler, PA **Type** R **Issue** '94 **OA** Kuskitannee #168
Description: This CSP is a return to the pre-25th anniversary patch. The design, by Chuck Day, incorporates the Council's Indian spirit. A fleur-de-lis sits within the rising sun. The paw on the canoe denotes Tiger Cubs, a boy's first Scouting experience. The "500" designates the Council's number. The eagle symbolizes the rank of Eagle Scout. The water, fields, and hills represent the fields and opportunities to explore as a Scout advances. The water, land, air, flora, and fauna of western Pennsylvania are also shown. The canoe brings Council youth into the Scouting community and offers them many opportunities to grow.
Scout_____ Date _____ Tel_____ E-mail _____

NORTHEASTERN PENNSYLVANIA Avoca, PA **Type** U **Issue** ____
_____**OA** Lowwapaneu #191
Description: On this CSP, Pennsylvania is outlined in red with the fleur-de-lis marking the Council's area, and the Susquehanna River flows through the Wyoming Valley. The region is noted for its woodlands, parks, and ski facilities, such as the pictured Montage Mountain.
Scout_____ Date _____ Tel_____ E-mail _____

PENN'S WOODS Armagh, PA **Type** U **Issue** '98 **OA** Nachamawat #275
Description: This patch symbolizes the area's industrial background. The coal bins represent the area's coal industry and the molten steel, the steel industry. In the forefront is a train, a reminder that Altoona, Pennsylvania, founded by the Pennsylvania Railroad, served as the base for the construction of a rail line across the Allegheny Mountains. The area is noted for its railroad repair and manufacturing shops. Some of the region's popular tourist attractions include an impressive railroad horseshoe curve and the Allegheny Portage Railroad National Historic Site. The train's searchlight shines a light on the Council's Scouting future. The Council's slogan, "Pathways to the Future," appears at the CSP's bottom. The green Alleghenies pictured represent the region's timber and agriculture businesses.
Scout_____ Date _____ Tel_____ E-mail _____

PENNSYLVANIA DUTCH Lancaster, PA **Type** U **Issue** ___ **OA** Wunita Gokhos #39
Description: This CSP depicts the beauty and simplicity of the Pennsylvania Dutch countryside, a misnomer since the majority of the Amish, Mennonite, and Brethren who settled here came from Germany, not the Netherlands. The German word for "German" (Deutsch) was mispronounced by the colonists as "Dutch," hence the name. The covered bridge represents the many covered bridges of the area. The longest and oldest is Mill Bridge. The barn, farmhouse, and farmlands symbolize the Pennsylvania Dutch's excellent farming skills. They are also known as the "Plain People" because of their simple manner of dress and lifestyle. The horse and buggy represent the extremely important role horses play in the lives of the Pennsylvania Dutch, who use them for transportation and farming
Scout_____ Date _____ Tel_____ E-mail _____

SUSQUEHANNA Williamsport, PA **Type** N **Issue** ____ **OA** Woapeu Sisilija #343
Description: The eagle soars past the yellow Indian arrowhead reminding us of the area and nation's great Indian heritage and Scouting's Order of the Arrow. The river and the Council's names, taken from the Susquehannock tribe, mean "Roily River." The Susquehanna flows through the Council's woodlands, creating a haven for wildlife and Scouts. The golden sun shines over the Scouting program. The area is the birthplace of Little League Baseball.
Scout_____ Date _____ Tel_____ E-mail _____

WESTMORELAND-FAYETTE Greensburg, PA **Type** U **Issue** '77 **OA** Wagion #6
Description: The two brown forts pictured are Fort Necessity on the right and Fort Ligonier on the left. Fort Necessity was the site of the beginning battle of the French and Indian War (The Battle of Great Meadows, July 3, 1754). It was also the site of George Washington's first major military campaign and the only surrender of his career. The fort is now a national Battlefield. Fort Ligonier was also a major English fortress used during the same war.
Scout_____ Date _____ Tel_____ E-mail _____

Pennsylvania - Puerto Rico - Rhode Island - South Carolina

YORK-ADAMS AREA York, PA **Type** N **Issue** _____ **OA** Tuckahoe #386
Description: CSP designer Robert Bennett wrote the following about his design: "The mountains in the background depict South Mountain, which is the eastern ridge of the Appalachian Mountains and the only part of the Appalachians which runs through Adams County. Camp Tuckahoe lies at the east of the ridge close to northern York County. The blue water represents the Conewago Creek whose headwaters begin in the mountains of Adams County and flow east through York County into the Susquehanna River. The first camp, Camp Ganoga, was established along the Conewago. The three tepees represent the three camps of York-Adams Area Council. The fleur-de-lis is the symbol of Scouting. The Boy Scout symbolizes the thousands of Scouts and Scouters who are, were, or will be members of Scouting in York-Adams Area Council, BSA."
Scout_____ Date _____ Tel_____ E-mail _____

PUERTO RICO San Juan, PR **Type** N **Issue** '98 **OA** Yokahu #506
Description: The fort represents Old San Juan, the historic section of the city. Here, one can find Fort San Geronimo, the San Juan National Historic Site with its El Morro and San Cristobal fortresses, La Fortaleza, the governor's palace, and Old Santo Domingo Convent. The birds and palm tree symbolize the rich wildlife and nature found on Puerto Rico, a U.S. Commonwealth since 1952. The "Isla del Encanto" translates from Spanish to mean "Island of Enchantment," Puerto Rico's nickname. The island is home to several thousand varieties of tropical plants. The Puerto Rico (Spanish for "Rich Port") flag also appears.
Scout_____ Date _____ Tel_____ E-mail _____

NARRAGANSETT Providence, RI **Type** N **Issue** 1/93 **OA** Wincheck #534
Description: Narragansett (Algonquian language) means "Calm Waters." It is the name of both the tribe that inhabited the area and the bay. The Narragansetts are called the "People of the Point." The Council includes areas in Rhode Island, Connecticut, and Massachusetts. The campfire represents the fires of troops past, present, and future. "YAWGOOG" is the name of a Narragansett chief and the Council's Scout camp. The large white feather is a tribute to the tribe. A single white feather was worn as a peace symbol. The two red stars are found on First Class Scout Badges and represent truth and knowledge.
Scout_____ Date _____ Tel_____ E-mail _____

BLUE RIDGE Greenville, SC **Type** U **Issue** _____ **OA** Atta Kulla Kulla #185
Description: The alluring Blue Ridge Mountains rise on this CSP, giving us a glimpse of the Cherokee Foothills and Paris Mountain State Park. The Cherokee Foothills Scenic Highway, one of the country's most beautiful, meanders through historic sites, lakes, and lush greenery. The Native American profile represents the Council's camp, Old Indian. Sassafras Mountain, the highest point in South Carolina, is located in Council territory.
Scout_____ Date _____ Tel_____ E-mail _____

COASTAL CAROLINA Charleston, SC **Type** U **Issue** _____ **OA** Un A Li'yi #236
Description: This patch is a rendition of the scenic South Carolina coast, which extends 187 miles. The Council includes the Outer Coastal Plain area, referred to as the "Low Country." A small chain of marshy islands, called "the Sea Islands," looks much like the scene on the patch. The two birds are egrets, found in great numbers along the shoreline. Charleston is one of the United States' busiest port cities. It is home to many colleges, including the College of Charleston (1770), the country's oldest municipal college (since 1837). Fort Sumter, Fort Moultrie, and Castle Pinckney all stand at the mouth of Charleston Harbor.
Scout_____ Date _____ Tel_____ E-mail _____

INDIAN WATERS Columbia, SC **Type** U **Issue** '99 **OA** Muscogee #221
Description: This new CSP was designed by Scout Executive, Michael R. Miller, who had this to say about his patch: "The navy blue background and white palmetto and moon are derived from the South Carolina State Flag. The crescent moon was worn on the hats of the Revolutionary War continentals who fought at Fort Moultrie against the British. The fort was made of palmetto logs. The Indian head signifies Indian Waters Council's rich Native American history with the Catawba, Edisto, Chrokee and Creek Indians. The logo and its compass points represent the future and its promise."
Scout_____ Date _____ Tel_____ E-mail _____

PALMETTO Spartanburg, SC **Type** U **Issue** '72 **OA** Skyuka #270
Description: A Palmetto, the state tree, is the centerpiece of this patch. It is surrounded by the Blue Ridge Mountains of upstate South Carolina. Above the Palmetto tree are the sun, the moon, and a star, emblematic of the South Carolina state flag and representative of the constancy of Scouting's purpose. In 1781, Spartanburg was the site of the Battle of Cowpens. This American Revolutionary War battle was a victory for the United States.
Scout_____ Date _____ Tel_____ E-mail _____

PEE DEE AREA Florence, SC **Type** U **Issue** _____ **OA** Santee #116
Description: Pee Dee refers to the largest Native American nation remaining in South Carolina. The Pee Dee River can be seen on this patch. The CSP contains images unique to this Council. The fowl is a gamecock, the symbol of the American Revolutionary War hero, Brigadier General Thomas Sumter. He was nicknamed "Gamecock of the Revolution" by the British because of his "hit and run" tactics. The city of Sumter was named in his honor. The Swamp Fox honors another American Revolutionary War General, Francis Marion. Marion would battle with the British and then disappear deep into the swamps, earning the name "Swamp Fox." The town of Marion and the 250,000-acre Francis Marion National Forest also bear his name. The pine trees represent the national forest. The crescent moon and the white Palmetto (state tree) are symbols also found on the South Carolina state flag.
Scout_____ Date _____ Tel_____ E-mail _____

South Dakota - Tennessee
V, A

BLACK HILLS AREA Rapid City, SD **Type** U **Issue** '99 **OA** Crazy Horse #171
Description: This patch is a slight variation on their last one, but with the same basic design.
It depicts the "Shrine of Democracy," Mt. Rushmore National Monument, and Scouting's
fleur-de-lis. Mt. Rushmore is located in the Black Hills Area Council. The blue sky glows
above the green forests of the Black Hills. The golden border and Scout emblem signify the
area's gold mines and the richness of the Scouting program. The Crazy Horse Memorial,
Badlands National Park, Devil's Tower National Monument, and Custer State Park are all
within the Council's territory.
Scout_____ Date _____ Tel_____ E-mail _____

SIOUX Sioux Falls, SD **Type** U **Issue** 1989 **OA** Tetonwana #105
Description: This CSP depicts Sioux Falls' prairie with the Missouri River running through
it. Shown are the Black Hills, which begin just past Council territory. The Sioux tepee
reminds us that the Sioux Indians inhabited this area before the arrival of the Europeans.
This Council covers several counties in three states: one in Iowa, seven in Minnesota, and
75 percent of the state of South Dakota. The famous Sioux writer, educator, and physician
Charles Eastman, also known as Ohiyesa (Sioux, "the Winner"), was involved with the BSA
from its onset and introduced Indian lore into Scouting.
Scout_____ Date _____ Tel_____ E-mail _____

CHICKASAW Memphis, TN **Type** U **Issue** 10/93 **OA** Ahoalan-Nachpikin #558
Description: This patch was issued after the merger of the Delta Area and Chickasaw Councils. Chickasaw is the Indian nation that inhabited the Chickasaw Bluffs of the Mississippi
River. Looking up the Mississippi River at twilight, the lights of Hernando de Soto Bridge
are seen connecting Tennessee and Arkansas. The cotton boll represents the main agricultural crop for this tri-state Council. Pictured in this CSP's background is Memphis' sports
and entertainment center, called the Great American Pyramid. This 321-foot tall building,
in the downtown riverfront area, is the largest pyramid ever built in the Americas. In the
foreground is a silhouette of a Scout giving the Scout Sign.
Scout_____ Date _____ Tel_____ E-mail _____

GREAT SMOKY MOUNTAIN Knoxville, TN **Type** U **Issue** '98 **OA** Pellissippi #230
Description: This patch depicts the state flag incorporated into a map of Tennessee. The
Council's territory is shown in white. The Council is home to the Great Smoky Mountains
National Park. The park is said to contain more varieties of plant life than the entire conti-
nent of Europe. The North American black bear pictured is native to the region. Dollywood
Theme Park, the Dixie Stampede, many country music theaters, the Knoxville Zoo, and the
Knoxville Museum of Art are all found in the Council's area.
Scout_____ Date _____ Tel_____ E-mail _____

N N

N N

N

CHEROKEE AREA Chattanooga, TN **Type** U **Issue** '99 **OA** Talidandaganu' #293
Description: *A Taste of Tennessee and the Grandeur of Georgia* are a pictorial series of CSPs depicting the famous landmarks that define the council's territory and commemorate the 90th anniversary of Scouting and the new millennium. Each CSP has a distinctive name and a unique story. **Unity** (top left) depicts the Tennessee, U.S., and Georgia flags as symbols of the Scouting ties that bind this Council together with one purpose and mission. **Point Park** (top right) is now a National Park on Lookout Mountain, overlooking the Tennessee River and the city of Chattanooga. This historic site housed Confederate artillery batteries used to protect this strategic location from Union armies. It was also the site of the famous "Battle Above the Clouds" (November 24, 1863), during which General Hooker and federal troops successfully overran Confederate forces who were hindered in their defense by dense fog that had settled on the mountain. **Heritage** (row two, left) features Chief John Ross and John Ross House. In the early 1800's, John Ross McDonald and Daniel Ross established a trading post on the Tennessee River at Ross's Landing, from which was born the city of Chattanooga, Tennessee. Daniel Ross's son, John, was elected chief of the Cherokees in the 1820's and served for 40 years. In 1838, he led his people on the infamous "Trail of Tears" march to the Oklahoma territory. **Nostalgia** (row two, right) depicts one of the 900 "See Rock City" barns that dotted the landscape from Michigan to Florida, starting in 1936. Famous for its "Fat Man Squeeze" and its view of seven states, this attraction draws thousands of visitors annually. **Skyline** (row three) is a collage of several distinctive and historic Chattanooga landmarks. The Tennessee River flows under the Walnut Street Bridge, the longest pedestrian bridge in the U.S. On the right is the Tennessee Aquarium, the world's largest freshwater aquarium. On the left is the "Chattanooga Choo-Choo," made famous by Glenn Miller. The railway was a major hub until the mid-1900's.

Scout_____ Date _____ Tel_____ E-mail _____
Scout_____ Date _____ Tel_____ E-mail _____
Scout_____ Date _____ Tel_____ E-mail _____
Scout_____ Date _____ Tel_____ E-mail _____
Scout_____ Date _____ Tel_____ E-mail _____

A

MIDDLE TENNESSEE Nashville, TN **Type** N **Issue** '99 **OA** Wa-Hi-Nasa #111
Description: The Council's new CSP celebrates the area's serenity and beauty. The lake pictured is Old Hickory Lake found at the Council's Camp Boxwell. Nashville is the home of the "Grand Ole Opry." This country music icon is the oldest continuous radio show in the United States. It airs live each week from the Opryland theater. The Middle Tennessee Council is the largest Council in Tennessee, serving 37 of the 95 counties in the state.
Scout_____ Date _____ Tel_____ E-mail _____

SEQUOYAH Johnson City, TN **Type** U **Issue** '93 **OA** Sequoyah #184
Description: This patch, designed by John Hurt, features the area's famous inhabitant Sequoyah (George Guess). He is shown with his traditional pipe, headdress, and neck medallion. The word on the left reads "Sequoyah" in the Cherokee alphabet, and on the right is the word "Council." Sequoyah developed this alphabet to preserve Cherokee culture. It took him 12 years to design this syllabary system, and he is the only person in history to develop an entire method of writing by himself (1809-1821). The CSP's black background represents night, and the sun's rays symbolize day. Places of interest in the Council's area include Bristol Caverns; Jonesborough—the oldest town in Tennessee; the Hands On! Museum; and Rocky Mount—once the capital of the U. S. south of the Ohio River (1790).
Scout_____ Date _____ Tel_____ E-mail _____

WEST TENNESSEE AREA Jackson, TN **Type** U **Issue** '97 **OA** Ittawamba #235
Description: This CSP's background is the state flag, and the state bird, the mockingbird, is also shown. John Luther "Casey" Jones, the legendary engineer of the Cannon Ball Express, lived in Jackson, and his home is now a railroad museum. Within the Council is Shiloh Military National Park, which memorializes one of the Civil War's bloodiest battles, the Battle of Shiloh. Almost a quarter of the 100,000 soldiers that fought the battle were either wounded or killed. Shiloh National Cemetery is the burial ground of 3,500 Union soldiers.
Scout_____ Date _____ Tel_____ E-mail _____

ALAMO AREA San Antonio, TX **Type** U **Issue** _____ **OA** Aina Topa Hutsi #60
Description: This CSP features the flag of Texas, the skyline of San Antonio, and the Alamo (the yellow building). This adobe building, once a Spanish mission, served as a fort in 1836. Here, Col. William Barrett Travis fought a gallant battle, attempting to gain Texas' independence from Mexico. Although 187 men died, including Davy Crockett and James Bowie, this small band of men kept Santa Anna's 4000 Mexican troops at bay for five days. Later, at the Battle of San Jacinto, where Santa Anna was finally defeated, the battle cry was "Remember the Alamo." This Council's name "Alamo Area" keeps the memory of this brave battle alive. The hot chili peppers represent the area's spicy foods and zest for life. The orange star-shaped design stands for Texas, the "Lone Star State."
Scout_____ Date _____ Tel_____ E-mail _____

M   B

BAY AREA Galveston, TX **Type** R **Issue** _____ **OA** Wihinipa Hinsa #113
Description: This patch features a sea gull soaring above the Gulf of Mexico and a dolphin jumping playfully through the blue waters. The city of Galveston is located on Galveston Island and is accessible via causeway, bridge, or boat. The area has long been a source of shrimp, as the depicted shrimp boat emphasizes. Galveston Bay, with its long beaches, is a popular tourist attraction. Shown on the patch is an oil rig. Rigs are found close to the shoreline, off-shore, and on land throughout the Council territory. Also pictured is the sun, which is rising and spreading its glow over the area's Scouts.
Scout_____ Date _____ Tel_____ E-mail _____

BUFFALO TRAIL Midland, TX **Type** U **Issue** _____ **OA** Tatanka #141
Description: The Council has returned to its pre-75th anniversary CSP. Buffalo Trail Council serves approximately 36,000 square miles of west Texas, including Big Bend National Park. The buffalo represents the herds of buffalo (American bison) that once roamed the west Texas plains. The bison were brought to the edge of extinction by white settlers who hunted them for sport and hides from 1830-1889. By 1889, the millions of buffalo had been reduced to about 1,000. Today about 30,000 bison exist on ranches and protected lands. The buffalo is standing on a golden path leading to the beautiful mountains of the area. The flowering yucca plants represent the flora of the Council's semi-desert area.
Scout_____ Date _____ Tel_____ E-mail _____

CADDO AREA Texarkana, TX **Type** U **Issue** _____ **OA** Akela Wahinapay #232
Description: This Council's name and CSP represent the Caddo Native Americans who lived in Texas, Arkansas, and Louisiana. The Caddo people had an agriculturally based society, engaging in farming and trading. The yellow background and green border symbolize corn, one of the major crops utilized by the area's tribes. The sacred pipe, or peace pipe, is the focal point of the patch. This pipe was used in a variety of different ceremonies. Also found on the CSP are a tomahawk (warclub), crossed arrows, and the BSA fleur-de-lis.
Scout_____ Date _____ Tel_____ E-mail _____

CAPITOL AREA Austin, TX **Type** U **Issue** '73 **OA** Tonkawa #99
Description: This Council, located in Texas' capital Austin, has designed its CSP in red, white, and blue. It features the Capitol Building and a single star representing Texas as the "Lone Star State." Prior to becoming the state capital, Austin was the capital of the Republic of Texas (1839-1842). Due to the many country-and-western musicians that have settled here, the city has earned the nickname, "The Live Music Capital of the World." Among the area's highlights are the Lyndon B. Johnson Library, which honors the Texas native and our 36th President, and the home of short story author William Sydney Porter, better known as O. Henry (1862-1910).
Scout_____ Date _____ Tel_____ E-mail _____

Texas

CHISHOLM TRAIL Abilene, TX **Type** N **Issue** '85 **OA** Kotso #330
Description: This Council derived its name from the historic Chisholm Trail. The trail was used after the American Civil War to lead cattle from San Antonio, Tx., through Indian Territory (now Oklahoma) to Abilene, Kansas. Abilene was the main destination for Texas cattle drives prior to the building of the Texas and Pacific railroad in 1881. The Council and trail were named for Jesse Chisholm, a Cherokee Native American who was a 19th Century guide and trader. The CSP, designed by Blake Woodall for the 1985 National Jamboree, depicts west Texas with longhorn cattle, buffalo (American Bison), a cowboy on horseback, cacti, wide-open spaces, and beautiful sunsets. Places to visit in the Council's area include Linear Air Park at Dyess Air Force Base, The Museums of Abilene, and the Abilene Zoo.
Scout_____ Date _____ Tel_____ E-mail _____

CIRCLE TEN Dallas, TX **Type** N **Issue** '99 **OA** Mikanakawa #101
Description: This new CSP is done in red, white, and blue, which is the same color scheme used on the state flag. The approximate location of the Council's headquarters is marked on the state by the golden fleur-de-lis. The lasso surrounding the state signifies the Council's western heritage. Originally the "Ten" in the Council's name stood for the ten counties that comprised the Council, but now it serves eleven Texas counties and one county in Oklahoma. The Dallas/Fort Worth region is part of the area known as the Metroplex. Some historic sites in Dallas include the National Historic Landmark, Fair Park—the world's largest art deco architecture and art district; Dealy Plaza, National Historic Landmark District—site of the 1963 assassination of President John F. Kennedy; and Old City Park.
Scout_____ Date _____ Tel_____ E-mail _____

COMANCHE TRAIL Brownwood, TX **Type** R **Issue** '79 **OA** Otena #295
Description: The arrowhead featured on this CSP was first used by the Council's Billy Gibbons Camp on their camp patch. The deer tracks across the center of the patch represent the Comanche Trail. The Council's name honors this trail and the nomadic Comanches. The steer head represents "The West" and one of the area's prime products—beef. The Council area contains the only suspension bridge still maintained by the highway department. Also located here are the Douglas MacArthur Academy of Freedom and Brownwood State Park.
Scout_____ Date _____ Tel_____ E-mail _____

CONCHO VALLEY San Angelo, TX **Type** R **Issue** '86 **OA** Wahinkto #199
Description: The magnificent western sunset glows in the background of this patch. The deer, symbolic of wildlife, and the Yucca plant, symbolic of the sparse desert plant life, are both pictured. The oil rig is a reminder of the rich black oil fields found within the area. The Council's name is taken from the Concho River and Fort Concho (now a museum), which are within the Council's territory.
Scout_____ Date _____ Tel_____ E-mail _____

A

EAST TEXAS AREA Tyler, TX **Type** U **Issue** '92 **OA** Tejas #72
Description: The white "Lone Star" represents the Texas nickname, the "Lone Star State." The blue sky represents the region's beautiful weather. The forest green symbolizes the pinewoods of east Texas, where forestry is a major industry. The blue stream below the forest represents the area's many lakes, streams, and rivers. The dark green at the bottom of the patch represents Tyler's fertile land and plant nursery industry. The city of Tyler, considered "The Rose Capital of the World," is well known for its field-grown rose bushes.
Scout_____ Date _____ Tel_____ E-mail _____

GOLDEN SPREAD Amarillo, TX **Type** U **Issue** ____ **OA** Nischa Achowalogen #486
Description: "Golden Spread" is a common term used in the Texas panhandle. It describes the vast areas of western Oklahoma, the Oklahoma and Texas panhandles, as well as eastern New Mexico. It also describes the ranch lands, grain farming, and long sunny days found here. The Council's patch depicts an Indian, a Boy Scout, and a military scout set against the background of the golden spread of the sun's rays. The soaring lone eagle heads towards a golden future. The word "Amarillo" means "yellow" in Spanish.
Scout_____ Date _____ Tel_____ E-mail _____

GULF COAST Corpus Cristi, TX **Type** U **Issue** '93 **OA** Karankawa #307
Description: This CSP represents the 17 counties of the Gulf Coast Council in south Texas. The longhorn skull depicts the area's ranching industry and history. The famous King Ranch is a part of the Council area, as are many other large ranches. The oil rig represents the historic and current oil industry, which is a major economic factor in southern Texas. The sailboat is the "Calamari," a winning race boat sailed by Explorer Troop Ship #1. The blue water represents the Council's location on the gulf, while the green turf reminds the viewer that Gulf Coast Council is still firmly planted in Texas' rich southern soil and history.
Scout_____ Date _____ Tel_____ E-mail _____

HEART O'TEXAS Waco, TX **Type** N **Issue** ____ **OA** Huaco #327
Description: This patch, designed by Hawkeye Roth, represents Waco and the Council's four districts. The tepees symbolize the Comanche Trail district and the region's strong Native American and frontier heritage. The Comanches, known for their expert horsemanship, lived in the area. Texas longhorn cattle represent the Chisholm Trail district. The trail, used by cowboys to herd cattle, traversed the area and ran from San Antonio, Tx., to Abilene, Kansas. The helicopter symbolizes the Leon Valley district, home of Fort Hood military base. The bridge crossing the Brazos River represents the Teha Lanna district and the area's many lakes and sparkling clean rivers. The bridge, built in 1870, was then one of the world's longest and led to the area's economic development.
Scout_____ Date _____ Tel_____ E-mail _____

Texas
N, A

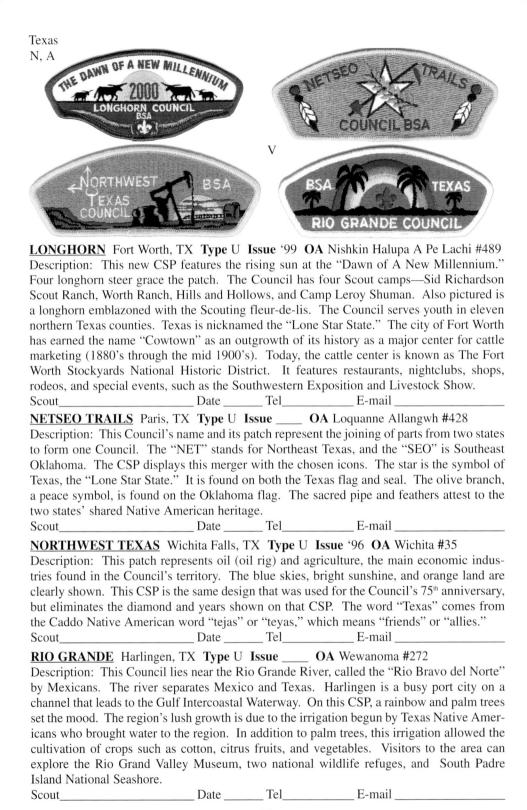

V

LONGHORN Fort Worth, TX **Type** U **Issue** '99 **OA** Nishkin Halupa A Pe Lachi #489
Description: This new CSP features the rising sun at the "Dawn of A New Millennium."
Four longhorn steer grace the patch. The Council has four Scout camps—Sid Richardson
Scout Ranch, Worth Ranch, Hills and Hollows, and Camp Leroy Shuman. Also pictured is
a longhorn emblazoned with the Scouting fleur-de-lis. The Council serves youth in eleven
northern Texas counties. Texas is nicknamed the "Lone Star State." The city of Fort Worth
has earned the name "Cowtown" as an outgrowth of its history as a major center for cattle
marketing (1880's through the mid 1900's). Today, the cattle center is known as The Fort
Worth Stockyards National Historic District. It features restaurants, nightclubs, shops,
rodeos, and special events, such as the Southwestern Exposition and Livestock Show.
Scout_____ Date _____ Tel_____ E-mail _____

NETSEO TRAILS Paris, TX **Type** U **Issue** _____ **OA** Loquanne Allangwh #428
Description: This Council's name and its patch represent the joining of parts from two states
to form one Council. The "NET" stands for Northeast Texas, and the "SEO" is Southeast
Oklahoma. The CSP displays this merger with the chosen icons. The star is the symbol of
Texas, the "Lone Star State." It is found on both the Texas flag and seal. The olive branch,
a peace symbol, is found on the Oklahoma flag. The sacred pipe and feathers attest to the
two states' shared Native American heritage.
Scout_____ Date _____ Tel_____ E-mail _____

NORTHWEST TEXAS Wichita Falls, TX **Type** U **Issue** '96 **OA** Wichita #35
Description: This patch represents oil (oil rig) and agriculture, the main economic industries found in the Council's territory. The blue skies, bright sunshine, and orange land are
clearly shown. This CSP is the same design that was used for the Council's 75th anniversary,
but eliminates the diamond and years shown on that CSP. The word "Texas" comes from
the Caddo Native American word "tejas" or "teyas," which means "friends" or "allies."
Scout_____ Date _____ Tel_____ E-mail _____

RIO GRANDE Harlingen, TX **Type** U **Issue** _____ **OA** Wewanoma #272
Description: This Council lies near the Rio Grande River, called the "Rio Bravo del Norte"
by Mexicans. The river separates Mexico and Texas. Harlingen is a busy port city on a
channel that leads to the Gulf Intercoastal Waterway. On this CSP, a rainbow and palm trees
set the mood. The region's lush growth is due to the irrigation begun by Texas Native Americans who brought water to the region. In addition to palm trees, this irrigation allowed the
cultivation of crops such as cotton, citrus fruits, and vegetables. Visitors to the area can
explore the Rio Grand Valley Museum, two national wildlife refuges, and South Padre
Island National Seashore.
Scout_____ Date _____ Tel_____ E-mail _____

M, A

SAM HOUSTON AREA Houston, TX **Type** U **Issue** _____ **OA** Colonneh #137
Description: This CSP bears the image of Sam Houston, the celebrated Texas hero. The Texas state flag serves as the patch's background. A Cherokee by adoption, Houston negotiated treaties to protect Native Americans from traders and represented the Cherokee Nation in Washington, DC. He fought for Texas' independence from Mexico in the Texas Revolution and served as Commander in Chief of the Texas Army. He was President of the Republic of Texas twice, and in 1845, when Texas joined the Union, he became one of its first senators. Houston is Texas' largest city and the fourth largest in the country. It is the center of the national petroleum industry. City sites include the Houston Museum of Fine Arts, Lyndon B. Johnson Space Center (NASA), and the Houston Zoo.
Scout_____ Date _____ Tel_____ E-mail _____
SOUTH PLAINS Lubbock, TX **Type** R **Issue** '89 **OA** Nakona #150
Description: This CSP depicts the southern portion of the Great Plains. This territory is called the Llano Estacado Plains meaning "Staked Plains." They were called this because the area was so difficult to travel through, stakes were planted to mark the paths. Found throughout the area are "mesas" (Spanish for tables), flat-topped rocks with steep cliffs for sides. The cowboy, twirling his lasso, symbolizes the area's cattle industry. Cotton is also a large industry of the region, with a great deal of it used for the production of denim jeans, a wardrobe staple for cowboys. Texas, with its "Lone Star," is shown on the left side in blue.
Scout_____ Date _____ Tel_____ E-mail _____
THREE RIVERS Beaumont, TX **Type** U **Issue** '98 **OA** Hasinai #578
Description: This patch pictures Texas in yellow with the state flag spreading out from the blue star, which represents the Council's area. The Council is bordered by the three rivers referred to by its name and on the CSP: the Neches, Trinity, and Sabine. The globe symbolizes the World Brotherhood of Scouting. Also pictured is an oil derrick, symbolic of the region's oil products. Beaumont is one of the country's largest petroleum refinery centers. The pine trees represent the timber industry. East Texas is known as "Piney Woods."
Scout_____ Date _____ Tel_____ E-mail _____
YUCCA El Paso, TX **Type** U **Issue** 1/93 **OA** Gila #378
Description: This Council is located near the border of Texas and New Mexico and encompasses areas in both states. The two Yucca plants (New Mexico's state flower) represent the two states. The patch also features the "Lone Star" of Texas and the ancient sun symbol of the Zia Pueblo Indians of New Mexico. The Franklin and Organ Mountains are shown in the background, and the desert floor is in the foreground. El Paso, meaning "The Pass" in Spanish, is the most important gateway city between Texas and Mexico. The city of Ciudad Juarez, Mexico, is linked both geographically and economically with El Paso.
Scout_____ Date _____ Tel_____ E-mail _____

A

M

GREAT SALT LAKE Salt Lake City, UT **Type** U **Issue** '99 **OA** El-Ku-Ta #520
Description: This new CSP features the same basic design, but the Council name has been enlarged and the oxen have changed colors. The Wasatch Mountains, which border Salt Lake City to the east, are shown in purple. The city skyline is black and depicts the capitol building, the Mormon Temple, and the urban mountain area. In the foreground is a covered wagon, led by oxen, representing the region's pioneer heritage. On the right are sea gulls, the state birds. The sky is orange for the great sunsets found in the area. The yellow and gold represent the Council's desert region.
Scout_____ Date _____ Tel_____ E-mail _____

TRAPPER TRAILS Ogden, UT **Type** R **Issue** 3/94 **OA** Awaxaawe' Awachia #535
Description: The Council adopted its name because this area was a prime location for hunting and trapping during the 1800's. The trapper in the center represents the many famous trappers, such as James Bridger, Peter Skene Ogden, and Miles Goodyear, who established the area's trading and helped settle the region. Shown are the Council vicinity's beautiful mountains, the cities of Ogden and Logan, and areas in Wyoming and Idaho that are a mountain man's paradise. The patch was designed by Rick Thomas of Logan, Utah.
Scout_____ Date _____ Tel_____ E-mail _____

UTAH NATIONAL PARKS Provo, UT **Type** U **Issue** ___ **OA** Tu-Cubin-Noonie #508
Description: Utah is the home of five magnificent national parks: Arches, Bryce Canyon, Canyonlands, Capitol Reef, and Zion. This colorful patch features Delicate Arch in Arches National Park. The park contains the world's largest concentration of natural stone arches (over 1,500). The dinosaur is a Diplodocus and represents Dinosaur National Monument. Many fossils and prehistoric animal bones were found in the area, including the remains of Apatosaurus and Allosaurus. The water represents the beautiful Yampa and Green Rivers and their canyons, as well as Lake Powell National Recreation Area. Also in the Council's domain lies Monument Valley, Utah. On this Navajo tribal land stand awesome maroon buttes and pinnacles, which rise 1,000-feet above the desert floor.
Scout_____ Date _____ Tel_____ E-mail _____

GREEN MOUNTAIN Waterbury, VT **Type** U **Issue** ____ **OA** Ajapeu #351
Description: Appropriately embroidered on a green background, this patch depicts one of the many covered bridges still in use in the Vermont countryside. The region's green trees and rolling mountains are also shown. The mountains' lush color is attributed to the densely packed spruce, pine, birch, sugar maple and beech trees. The outline of the state can be found in gray in the lower left of the patch. The Green Mountains, which extend through the length of Vermont, afford Scouts and tourists the chance to enjoy magnificent scenery, camping, picnicking, and hiking.
Scout_____ Date _____ Tel_____ E-mail _____

N, A

VIRGIN ISLANDS St. Thomas, VI **Type** U **Issue** _____ **OA** Arawak #562
Description: The U.S. Virgin Islands, part of the Lesser Antilles chain of the West Indies, are located between the Caribbean Sea and the Atlantic Ocean. Pictured are the three main islands—St. Thomas, St. Croix and St. John. St. John, the smallest island, has 75% of its land devoted to the Virgin Islands National Park. Here, visitors will find Native American petroglyphs (rock carvings) and beautiful coral reefs. St. Croix is the eastern most point under the U. S. flag. St. Thomas contains the territorial capital of the U.S. Virgin Islands, Charlotte Amalie. The island was a favorite hideout of Captain Kidd, Blackbeard, and Bluebeard. It is also home to the second oldest Jewish synagogue in the Western Hemisphere.
Scout_____ Date _____ Tel_____ E-mail _____

BLUE RIDGE MOUNTAINS Roanoke, VA **Type** N **Issue** _____ **OA** Tutelo #161
Description: The glorious Blue Ridge Mountains, topped with snow, are featured on this CSP. The blue water represents Smith Mountain Lake and Claytor Lake, favorite-fishing grounds for the locals. The lush green fields symbolize the meadows, farmlands, and farmers' markets found in the Council's service area. The golden sun is shown reflecting on the water, representing a new day of Scouting. The city of Roanoke was once known as "Big Lick," a reference to the nearby salt licks.
Scout_____ Date _____ Tel_____ E-mail _____

COLONIAL VIRGINIA Newport News, VA **Type** R **Issue** '99 **OA** Wahunsenakah #333
Description: The patriotic theme of this new CSP denotes this Virginia area's role as the "Cradle of Democracy." Virginia, the tenth of the original thirteen states, is shown in green. From left to right, the flags pictured are the British Union Jack, the U.S. flag, and the flag of the original thirteen colonies. The building depicted is Colonial Williamsburg's capitol. The ship represents the one that brought the English colonists to Jamestown, the first American colony (1607). At Colonial Williamsburg and Colonial National Historical Park, Jamestown, visitors may witness actors re-creating colonial life.
Scout_____ Date _____ Tel_____ E-mail _____

ROBERT E. LEE Richmond, VA **Type** R **Issue** _____ **OA** Nawakwa #3
Description: This CSP pictures Virginia with the Council territory in red. Also shown are the state flower—the flowering dogwood, and the state bird—the cardinal. The Council name honors Robert E. Lee, the Commander in Chief of Virginia's military and naval forces, and later, of the Confederate armies. Richmond was the capital of the Confederacy throughout most of the American Civil War (1861-1865). Area attractions include the Edgar Allan Poe Museum, the State Capitol (designed by Thomas Jefferson), Monument Avenue, and Hollywood Cemetery. The cemetery contains the graves of U.S. Presidents James Monroe and John Tyler, Confederate President John Marshall, and 18,000 Confederate soldiers.
Scout_____ Date _____ Tel_____ E-mail _____

Virginia - Washington

M

N, M

N

SHENANDOAH AREA Winchester, VA **Type** N **Issue** 10/94 **OA** Shenshawpotoo #276
Description: This Council is located in the Shenandoah Valley, as outlined on the CSP. The apple represents the vast apple industry found in this orchard region of Virginia and West Virginia. The cannon symbolizes the historic part the city of Winchester played as the site for three important Civil War battles. In 1748, George Washington began his surveying career in Winchester. He also had an office here, which he used while building Fort Loudoun (1755-1756). "Stonewall" Jackson's Headquarters are here as well (1861-1862). Winchester is the birthplace of author Willa Cather and Admiral Richard E. Byrd.
Scout_____ Date _____ Tel_____ E-mail _____

STONEWALL JACKSON AREA Waynesboro, VA **Type** N **Issue** '88

OA Shenandoah #258
Description: This Council's name and patch honor Thomas Jonathan "Stonewall" Jackson, a Confederate general who fought in the Shenandoah Valley and Upper Piedmont region of Virginia. Jackson's campaigns were waged in the territories that surround the Council. Jackson received his nickname at the First Battle of Bull Run (1861), where it was reported Jackson and his troops stood against the Union Army "like a stone wall."
Scout_____ Date _____ Tel_____ E-mail _____

TIDEWATER Virginia Beach, VA **Type** N **Issue** ____ **OA** Blue Heron #349
Description: Tidewater Council incorporates regions of Virginia and North Carolina. This CSP features a naval ship, representing the region's importance as a military center. The area has one of the world's largest concentrations of naval installations. Military bases include the Norfolk Naval Shipyard, Dam Neck Naval Base, Oceana Naval Air Station, Little Creek Naval Amphibious Base, and Fort Story U. S. Army Base. The sailing ship denotes the area's past and present history as a major seaport. Also pictured is the Cape Hatteras lighthouse on the North Carolina outer banks. It lights the way for ships sailing around "the Graveyard of the Atlantic." The ship's wheel is the Council's logo. Some area places of interest include: Nauticus—the National Maritime Center; Kitty Hawk, N.C.,—where Orville and Wilber Wright's historic first flight took place; and the Virginia Beach resorts.
Scout_____ Date _____ Tel_____ E-mail _____

BLUE MOUNTAIN Kennewick, WA **Type** U **Issue** '99 **OA** Wa-La-Moot-Kin #336
Description: This new, unusually shaped patch features the Blue Mountains, which extend into Washington and Oregon. The mountains, referred to as "the Blues" by the locals, also represent Mt. Rainer (Washington) and Mt. Hood (Oregon). The trees symbolize Washington's nickname, "the Evergreen State." The wagon wheel and skull represent the Oregon Trail. The square or "joining" knot depicts the joining of the two states by the Council. The square knot is also the first knot a Boy Scout learns upon joining the BSA.
Scout_____ Date _____ Tel_____ E-mail _____

CHIEF SEATTLE Seattle, WA **Type** U **Issue** ____ **OA** T'Kope Kwiskwis #502
Description: The city and Council were named for the friendly Suquamish (a tribe of the northwest coast Native Americans) leader Sealth, or Chief Seattle. This patch's bright red background is overlaid with a Native American drawing of whales. Located on the Pacific Ocean and Puget Sound, fishing and whaling were important trades for the Native Americans. The waterways were also used as main travel routes. Seattle, Washington's most populous city, was the gateway for the Yukon and Alaska goldrushes of the 1890's. The city is home to the Seattle Center, which was the site of the 1962 world's fair, The Century 21 Exposition. The 607-foot high Space Needle, built for the fair, houses a revolving restaurant and an observation deck that allows a panoramic view of the city. The area is also home to jetplane manufacturer, The Boeing Company, and computer software giant, Microsoft.
Scout_____ Date _____ Tel_____ E-mail _____

GRAND COLUMBIA Yakima, WA **Type** N **Issue** ____ **OA** Tataliya #614
Description: Once known as the Oregon River, the Columbia River is 1,245 miles long and the longest western river. It passes through a small part of the Council and is depicted on the CSP. The snow covered Cascade Mountains are home to the Council's camp. This area of the Cascades includes two volcanoes, Mt. Adam and the Cascades' highest peak—Mt. Rainier (14,410-feet). This region is known as the "Apple Capital of the World." One of the largest Indian Nations in the U.S., the Yakima Nation, also calls this area home. The pine trees symbolize the region's forestlands, parks, and vineyards.
Scout_____ Date _____ Tel_____ E-mail _____

INLAND NORTHWEST Spokane, WA **Type** U **Issue** '93 **OA** Es Kaielgu #311
Description: This Council's name honors the "Northwest Inland Empire," a name given to the area by Lewis and Clark in the 1800's. Mt. Spokane, which is covered by snow seven months of the year, is featured. The Spokane River, which flows northwest into Long Lake, is also shown. The tents and the trees symbolize the Council's three camps: Camp Cowles, Camp Easton, and Camp Grizzly. The trees also represent the Spokane State Forestlands and the region's many national parks. The gold tree is a fir without needles, or a snag.
Scout_____ Date _____ Tel_____ E-mail _____

MOUNT BAKER Everett, WA **Type** N **Issue** ____ **OA** Sikhs Mox Lamonti #338
Description: Pictured is the Council's namesake, Mt. Baker. It is part of the Cascade Range and soars to a height of 10,775-feet. The green hills and Western Hemlock trees (the state tree) symbolize the region's vast forestlands. The Orca whale represents the schools (pods) that frequent this area in winter. Visitors can take Orca sighting cruises from Friday Harbor or visit the Boeing 747-767-777 Production Facility to learn how an airplane is built. The totem pole represents the handiwork of Northwest Coast Native Americans.
Scout_____ Date _____ Tel_____ E-mail _____

N

PACIFIC HARBORS Tacoma, WA **Type** U **Issue** 12/92 **OA** Nisqually #155
Description: This CSP was created when Twin Harbors, Tumwater, and Mt. Rainier Councils merged. The blue and white represent the waters of Puget Sound. The green field represents the lush foliage found in the forests of the Cascade and Olympic Mountain ranges. The symbolic lighthouse stands guard at Tacoma, Olympia, and Aberdeen harbors. Mt. Rainier, seen throughout this Council, is pictured with the sun rising. The sun hints at the bright new beginnings of this Council. Mt. Rainier National Park and Olympic National Park are within the Council's service area.
Scout_____ Date _____ Tel_____ E-mail _____

ALLOHAK Parkersburg, WV **Type** N **Issue** ____ **OA** Nendawen #618
Description: This Council's name is taken from the Native American word meaning "Great Mighty One." The Council spans areas in Ohio and West Virginia. The shapes of Ohio (dark green) and West Virginia (light green) are seen above the blue Ohio River. The beautiful Blue Ridge Mountains, with the colorful sun setting behind them, symbolize the area's many forestlands. An area highlight is Blennerbassett Island Park. This is the place where Aaron Burr (our third Vice President) and Harman Blennerbassett plotted unsuccessfully to seize land to form a new republic (1805).
Scout_____ Date _____ Tel_____ E-mail _____

BUCKSKIN Charleston, WV **Type** N **Issue** ____ **OA** Chi-Hoota-Wei #617
Description: This Council's new patch was selected from among the many designs submitted by the Council's Scouts and Scouters. It features Dilly's Mill, which can be found at the Council's camp. The Council represents Scouts from areas in the three states noted at the bottom of the CSP (West Virginia, Virginia, and Kentucky). The Council's number, "617," is embroidered on the golden sun shown at the end of the path. Charleston is the capital of West Virginia and its largest city. The city hosts two annual events: the Vandalia Gathering (Memorial Day weekend) and the Charleston Sternwheel Regatta (Labor Day weekend).
Scout_____ Date _____ Tel_____ E-mail _____

MOUNTAINEER AREA Fairmont, WV **Type** R **Issue** '99 **OA** Menawngihella #550
Description: This new CSP is a blue and green version of the one designed by Ken Shanes, the Council's Scout Executive. Pictured are the lush green lands and the deep green scenic mountains found throughout West Virginia. In fact, the city name of Fairmont is a contraction of "fair mountain." The Mountaineer stands proudly and represents the early mountaineers who settled here. He is also the logo of the University of West Virginia. Fairmont is the industrial center of a coal-mining region and is home to the first commercial coal mine (1811). Area attractions include Prickett's Fort State Park and Cooper's Rock State Forest.
Scout_____ Date _____ Tel_____ E-mail _____

B

OHIO RIVER VALLEY Wheeling, WV **Type** U **Issue** 1991 **OA** Onondaga #36
Description: This patch depicts the Ohio River that runs through the Council's center and borders Ohio and West Virginia's northern panhandle. Pictured is the suspension bridge on the National Road that links the two states. On the left is the first Federal Land Grant Office at Steubenville, Ohio. On the right are West Virginia's beautiful green hills and the steel melting pot, which represents the steel-making industries of the valley. The cardinal, the state bird of both states, is also pictured. This design comes from a contest won by Boy Scout Scott Sliva.
Scout_____ Date _____ Tel_____ E-mail _____
TRI-STATE AREA Huntington, WV **Type** U **Issue** _____ **OA** Thal-Coo-Zyo #457
Description: On this CSP, each point of land is marked as one of the three states that make up the Council and the region: Ohio, Kentucky, and West Virginia. The barge floats down the Ohio River (Algonquian for "Beautiful River"), which is common ground for all three states. A bridge is seen spanning the shores from Ohio to West Virginia, uniting the two states. The bright sun shines over Scouting throughout the region.
Scout_____ Date _____ Tel_____ E-mail _____
BAY LAKES Menasha, WI **Type** U **Issue** '71 **OA** Awase #61
Description: The Council's 25th anniversary CSP has been retired, and the Council has returned to its previous patch. The "Lakes" and "Bay" of the Bay Lakes Council refer to Lake Michigan, Lake Winnebago, and Green Bay. The patch symbolizes northeastern Wisconsin with its many lakes and forest areas, such as the Kettle Moraine area and the Nicolet National Forest. There are three hills and three trees, each symbolizing one of the six Councils that merged to make Bay Lakes Council. The Council area is home to the championship Green Bay Packers football team. The Green Bay Packer Hall of Fame museum traces the history of the team. The Packers are the oldest professional football team in the National Football League. Another interesting site in the area is the National Railroad Museum. Here, visitors can take a one-mile ride aboard a 1910 standard-gauge train and see a multimedia show, "Rails to America."
Scout_____ Date _____ Tel_____ E-mail _____
CHIPPEWA VALLEY Eau Claire, WI **Type** U **Issue** '78 **OA** Otyokwa #337
Description: This patch represents the four districts (Golden Eagle, White Pine, Blue Hills, and Silver Waters) that were combined to form this new Council. The golden eagle, white pine trees, blue hills, and silver waters are all pictured on this CSP. The magnificent effects of the sun may also be seen, rising over the Council territory. The Chippewa Native Americans, the original settlers of the valley, have been honored by the naming of this region and this Council.
Scout_____ Date _____ Tel_____ E-mail _____

FOUR LAKES Madison, WI **Type** U **Issue** '99 **OA** Tichora #146
Description: This new patch was designed by Tony Lazewski. The "Four Lakes" referred
to by the Council's name are the Mendota, Monana, Wingra, and Waubesa Lakes. The State
Capitol dome is pictured. Madison, the state capital, was named for President James Madison. Within the black circle is the state of Wisconsin, "America's Dairyland." This center
icon was taken from Wisconsin's official sesquicentennial celebration. The original icon
contained the dates 1848-1998. The canoeist represents the area's Native American heritage.
The Ho Chunks (Winnabagos) are local inhabitants. The lakes are the region's primary
source of recreation. They support a variety of water sports and contain many scenic vistas.
Scout_____ Date _____ Tel_____ E-mail _____

GATEWAY AREA La Crosse, WI **Type** U **Issue** '99 **OA** Ni-Sanak-Tani #381
Description: La Crosse, Wisconsin, is known as the "Northern Gateway to the West," hence,
the Council's name. This new CSP is reminiscent of the Scout Badge. The trefoil, plus the
eagle and shield, sit atop the patriotic colored ribbon. The two stars at either side complete
the badge effect. The white lines above the trefoil depict the area's bluffs. This area of Wisconsin was spared when the last great glaciers passed through 10,000 years ago. This "Driftless" area's steep and rugged landscape gave the region the nickname "Bluff Country." The
white curvy line below the trefoil represents the Mississippi River. The river forms more
than half of western Wisconsin's border with its neighboring states, Minnesota and Iowa.
Scout_____ Date _____ Tel_____ E-mail _____

MILWAUKEE Milwaukee, WI **Type** U **Issue** ____ **OA** Mikano #231
Description: Milwaukee is a major port on the Great Lakes and St. Lawrence Seaway. The
Council and city's names are from the Potawatomi term "Mahn-ah-wauk," which means
"Gathering Place by the Water." The CSP stresses the Council's water connection. Shown
are the blue waters, the ship's wheel—representing the Port of Milwaukee, and the Hoen
Bridge, which spans the harbor. Also pictured, in white, is the city's skyline. The city, synonymous with beer, was home to some of the country's leading breweries. Many of the
buildings, sports teams, and recreation areas have names reflecting the industry's influence.
Scout_____ Date _____ Tel_____ E-mail _____

POTAWATOMI AREA Waukesha, WI **Type** U **Issue** '97 **OA** Wag-O-Shag #280
Description: This Council's name honors the Potawatomi Native Americans, also known as
the Fire Nation. Their name means "People of the Place of Fire" in Algonquian. A
Potawatomi is pictured canoeing down one of the area's lakes. A bright orange sun reflects
upon the water. The tribe helped develop the Dream Dance, a dance of goodwill towards all
men. The Council is located in Waukesha, which means "By the Little Fox" (Potawatomi).
The city has many mineral springs and was a famous health resort from 1868 until 1915.
Scout_____ Date _____ Tel_____ E-mail _____

SAMOSET Wausau, WI **Type** U **Issue** '98 **OA** Tom Kita Chara #96
Description: This CSP, designed by Bruce Mickelson, features "Smiley the Tent." Smiley
was drawn for the Council by Walt Disney in 1953. The symbolism of the patch is "When
you say "Samoset," you have said it all!" The dark green background symbolizes the area's
trees. This region of north central Wisconsin had a history of lumberjacking and logging,
but the area is now a pioneer in the reforestation of land devastated by the logging practices
of the 19th century. The Council's name honors Chief Samoset ("He Who Walks Over
Much," Abenaki dialect), the first person who greeted the Plymouth Pilgrims. Samoset
spoke English and surprised the Pilgrims with the phrase, "Welcome, Englishmen!"
Scout_____ Date _____ Tel_____ E-mail _____

SINNISSIPPI Janesville, WI **Type** U **Issue** '99 **OA** Chemokemon #226
Description: This new patch was designed by Jenny Bevans. The Council, located in southern Wisconsin on the Rock River, was formed when the Stateline and Indian Trails Councils
merged in 1966. The CSP's night scene features the on-going theme of a Native American
canoeist traveling down the Rock River. The canoeist has appeared on every one of the
Council's patches. He represents the many Mississippi Valley Native American cultures.
Scout_____ Date _____ Tel_____ E-mail _____

SOUTHEAST WISCONSIN Racine, WI **Type** U **Issue** '71 **OA** Mascoutens #8
Description: This CSP features a loon flying above Lake Michigan. The scene is reminiscent of the view from the mouth of the Root River. Lake Michigan and the Root River are
located in the Council's area. The city's name, Racine, is the French word for "root." The
name was given to the area because of the many roots found along the riverbank. This is
also the reason why the river was named the Root River. The name Wisconsin is the French
version of the Ojibwa (also known as Chippewa) term meaning "Gathering of the Waters"
or "Place of the Beaver."
Scout_____ Date _____ Tel_____ E-mail _____

CENTRAL WYOMING Casper, WY **Type** U **Issue** '97 **OA** Tatokainyanka #356
Description: This patch, designed by Lee Patterson, features both an antelope and the
famous geyser, Old Faithful. The antelope is the totem of the Council's OA lodge. Although
Yellowstone National Park, where Old Faithful is located, is not a part of any Council, Central Wyoming Council's Camp Buffalo Bill is situated just 11 miles from Yellowstone's eastern gate. Independence Rock State Historic Site is found within the Council area. Independence Rock is a 193-foot high granite boulder that covers 27 acres at its base. It is also
called "The Great Register of the Desert." Carved on the boulder are the names of over
5,000 explorers, scientists, soldiers, trappers, emigrants, and adventurers of old who left their
marks as they stopped here in their travels.
Scout_____ Date _____ Tel_____ E-mail _____

N

DIRECT SERVICE AROUND THE WORLD Irving, Texas **Type** U **Issue** _____
OA Gamenowinink #555
Description: The Direct Service Council brings the Boy Scouts of America to American youth located in foreign countries. The Scouts served are the dependents of U.S. military, embassy, State Department, or business people based overseas. The symbol in the center of the patch represents Scouting's presence, which spans the globe. A service star and a fleur-de-lis flank each side of the CSP and act as reminders of the Scouting program. The countries served by the Direct Service Council include: Argentina, Egypt, Guatemala, Hong Kong, Indonesia, Kenya, Panama, Russia, Saudi Arabia, Singapore, and Venezuela.
Scout_____ Date _____ Tel_____ E-mail _____

DIRECT SERVICE ARGENTINA Irving, Texas **Type** U **Issue** _____ **OA** _____ #__
Description: This Council's patch features the flag of the U.S. and part of the Argentine flag. The actual Argentine flag has the "Sun of May" in its center. The "Sun of May" emblem represents the sun that shone over the May 1810 demonstration against Spanish rule. This was the first of many such uprisings that finally culminated in Argentina's independence (1816). The symbol in the middle of the patch is a variation of the International Scouting emblem. Argentina is the second largest country in South America. Buenos Aires is the country's largest city and its capital.
Scout_____ Date _____ Tel_____ E-mail _____

DIRECT SERVICE EGYPT Irving, Texas **Type** U **Issue** _____ **OA** _____ # __
Description: The Egyptian Council's CSP design is oriented towards the areas near Cairo and Upper Egypt. It depicts the pyramids at Giza, the country's desert area, a dromedary or Arabian camel (one hump), and a felucca (ship) with the BSA fleur-de-lis on its sail, floating down the Nile River. The Arab Republic of Egypt is over 90 percent desert. Its desert areas include the Libyan Desert (or Western Desert), a part of the Sahara Desert, and the Arabian Desert (or Eastern Desert). The country's capital and largest city is Cairo. Less than one-tenth of Egypt's land is settled.
Scout_____ Date _____ Tel_____ E-mail _____

DIRECT SERVICE EGYPT-ALEXANDRIA-LONE SCOUTS Irving, Texas **Type** N
Issue '99 **OA** __
Description: This CSP, designed by Philip Ian Tristan Abbey, is an adaptation of the Alexandria Governorate's flag. Pictured is one of the Seven Wonders of the Ancient World—the Pharos Lighthouse at Alexandria. The 384-foot high (about 38 floors) lighthouse shone its light for over 1,300 years before suffering damage during a series of earthquakes between 1100 and 1400 AD. In the late 15th century, Quit Bey Fortress was built over the lighthouse's former site. Today, the lighthouse is a city icon, appearing on many official logos.
Scout_____ Date _____ Tel_____ E-mail _____

DIRECT SERVICE GUATEMALA Irving, Texas **Type** U **Issue** _____ **OA** _____ # __
Description: Guatemala is Central America's third largest country and its most populated.
The capital and largest city is Guatemala City. The volcano pictured is most likely Taju-
mulco Volcano. At 13,845-feet, it is the country's highest point. Guatemala has 19 active
volcanoes. The country is also prone to earthquakes. Most of the nation's people are Mayan
Native Americans or Ladinos (Spanish for Latins). The Mayans, an advanced culture, used
hieroglyphics, had sophisticated scientific knowledge, and followed a complex calendar system. A 3rd and 4th Century Mayan ruin may be visited in Tikal, Guatemala.
Scout_____Date _____ Tel_____ E-mail _____
DIRECT SERVICE HONG KONG Irving, Texas **Type** U **Issue** _____ **OA** _____ # __
Description: Hong Kong, a region of China, is located off China's southeast coast. It is
made up of Hong Kong Island, the mainlands of Kowloon and the New Territories, and over
200 small islands. From 1840 until 1997, Hong Kong was under British rule. On July 1,
1997, Hong Kong reverted back to China and became the Hong Kong Special Administra-
tion Region (SAR). This CSP features the sun glowing behind Hong Kong and a junk (a
Chinese fishing boat) floating on the South China Sea. Fishing is an important industry for
Hong Kong. Hong Kong Island is home to most government offices and is one of the world's
most important financial centers as well. Kowloon is the urban administrative area, a major
manufacturing center, and the site of many parks, museums, and tourist attractions.
Scout_____Date _____ Tel_____ E-mail _____
DIRECT SERVICE INDONESIA Irving, Texas **Type** U **Issue** _____ **OA** _____ # __
Description: Pictured are the north and south island strings that comprise the Republic of
Indonesia. The major islands are Sumatra, Java, and Timor on the north string and Sulawe-
si, Moluccas (Spice Islands), and New Guinea on the south. This island republic of Southeast Asia was ruled by the Dutch from the 1600's until 1945. It is the world's fourth most
populated country, with over half the people residing on Java. Jakarta, on Java, is the country's capital and largest city. The blue area represents the South China Sea, the Celebes Sea,
the Pacific Ocean, and the Indian Ocean. The red and white are the colors of the Indonesian
flag. The red symbolizes gallantry and freedom; the white stands for justice and purity.
Scout_____Date _____ Tel_____ E-mail _____
DIRECT SERVICE KENYA Irving, Texas **Type** U **Issue** _____ **OA** _____ # __
Description: Kenya's CSP features two African elephants, which represent the area's wide
variety of wildlife and big game. Also shown is Mount Kenya, an extinct volcano, which at
17,058 feet, is the second highest mountain in Africa. Nairobi is the nation's capital and
largest city. The National Museum of Kenya, the Sorsbie Art Gallery, and Nairobi National Park are major tourist attractions in Nairobi.
Scout_____Date _____ Tel_____ E-mail _____

Direct Service
B

DIRECT SERVICE SAUDI ARABIA Irving, Texas **Type** U **Issue** ____ **OA** ____ **#** __
Description: This return CSP features the kingdom of Saudi Arabia's yellow deserts, a palm
tree, and two camels. Over half of the country is desert. The Great Sandy Desert covers
much of the southeast, while part of the Syrian Desert extends into the north. Camels are
used as beasts of burden and in caravans traveling across the desert because of their strength,
endurance, and low water requirements. Camel racing is a popular sporting event. Riyadh
is Saudi Arabia's capital city and its most populated one as well. Other important cities
include Mecca—destination of the annual Muslim pilgrimage; Medina—the holy city for the
Islamic people; and Ad Dammān—an oil center on the Persian Gulf. The palm tree represents a desert oasis and dates, an important crop for the country. The green used on the CSP
is the same color used on the Saudi Arabian flag. The Saud family has used the green banner of Islam since the 1700's.
Scout_____ Date _____ Tel_____ E-mail _____
DIRECT SERVICE SINGAPORE Irving, Texas **Type** U **Issue** ____ **OA** _____ **#** __
Description: Singapore is an independent city-state consisting of one main island and 50
adjacent islands. The majority of the people are Chinese, but there are Malay and Indian
minorities as well. Singapore is an important manufacturing hub and financial center in
Southeast Asia. The ship on the patch is either a Chinese junk or a Portugese lorcha, either
of which denotes Singapore's maritime history and renown as a world port and trade center.
The blue water represents the Johor and Singapore Straits. Pictured is a "merlion," a lion
head on a mermaid's tail. The merlion is the symbol of Singapore, "the Lion City." The lettering used to spell out the name "Singapore" is the same one used by the Singapore Tourist
Promotion Board. The tourist board also uses the merlion as its logo.
Scout_____ Date _____ Tel_____ E-mail _____
DIRECT SERVICE VENEZUELA Irving, Texas **Type** U **Issue** ____ **OA** _____ **#** __
Description: This CSP and the fleur-de-lis on the left utilize the colors of the Venezuelan
flag. The yellow represents the land, the blue symbolizes the ocean, and red represents the
blood of patriots. The center symbol represents World Scouting. The knot symbolizes the
strength and unity of the world brotherhood of Scouting. The royal purple stands for leadership and helpfulness. Caracas is the country's capital city and its commercial, financial,
and cultural center. Caracas is also home to the Bolivar Museum. The museum features displays and information about Simón Bolívar, the South American revolutionary, military
leader, and politician. Bolívar is known as the "Liberator" for his leading role in the wars
for Spanish American Independence. Venezuela was named in 1499 by Spanish explorer
Alonso de Ojeda. The region, studded with Native American buildings perched on stilts
along the edge of Lake Maracaibo, reminded Ojeda of Venice, Italy.
Scout_____ Date _____ Tel_____ E-mail _____

N  N

FAR EAST Tokyo, Japan **Type** N **Issue** '99 **OA** Achpateuny #498
Description: This new CSP is similar to the former one, however the shape of each nation
has changed slightly. The Council serves the youth of U.S. military, diplomatic, and business people stationed in the Western Pacific area and in Asia. It is broken into three districts: Japan, Great Okinawa, and Korea. Pictured are the nations the Council now serves
or has served at one time. Shown in red are Japan and the Okinawa district. The yellow
area is Korea. The green region represents the Philippines and Taiwan. Thailand is featured
in violet. The dark blue symbolizes the rest of Asia, and the white is the ocean. The star
represents both the sun and a compass rose. Japan is known as "The Land of the Rising
Sun." This name comes from the country's Japanese name, Dai Nippon, which means
"Great Origin of the Sun." The sun has been the country's and the emperor's symbol since
at least the 14th century. Tokyo is Japan's capital and largest city. Okinawa was a separate
kingdom prior to the 14th century. It then paid tribute to China until Japan annexed it in 1879.
As a result of World War II, the U.S. maintained control of Okinawa from 1945 to 1972, at
which time it was returned to Japan. The U.S. military now leases land from Okinawa
landowners but is scheduled to give back 20 percent of this occupied land by 2001. In 1948,
Korea was divided into two nations at the 38th parallel: North Korea (Democratic People's
Republic of Korea) and South Korea (Republic of Korea). South Korea is a democratic
republic. Seoul is its capital and largest city. North Korea is a communist state. Pyongyang
is its largest city and capital. The U.S. has had a military presence in Korea since 1945. The
Far East Council can claim alumni from almost every other BSA council.
Scout_____ Date _____ Tel_____ E-mail _____

TRANSATLANTIC Germany **Type** N **Issue** '99 **OA** Black Eagle #482
Description: The Council's new patch celebrates some of the countries that host its Scout
Troops. The Council was formed in May of 1950, at which time it served United States
Army dependents in Germany and Austria. In 1959, the BSA assigned the Council juris-
diction over U.S. government installations and military facilities in Europe, the Near East,
and North Africa, including Ethiopia. The Transatlantic Council (TAC) is the largest Coun-
cil in landmass in the Boy Scouts of America. These countries change from time to time,
and there are plans to expand and reclaim countries supported by the Council in the past.
The patch features the flags of most of the host nations. The top row, from left to right, has
the following flags: Poland, France, the Netherlands, Italy, Germany, United States, United
Kingdom, Belgium, Greece, and Austria. On the bottom row, left to right, are the flags of
Turkey, the Czech Republic, Luxembourg, Morocco, Hungry, Portugal, Spain, and Switzer-
land. Also part of TAC, but not represented on the patch, are the countries of Andorra, Russia, Finland, and Croatia. Several different branches of the United States military partici-
pate in the Transatlantic Council. They are the United States Air Force in Europe (USAFE),
the United States Army in Europe (USAREUR), and Navy Europe (NAVEUR).
Scout_____ Date _____ Tel_____ E-mail _____

MILLENNIUM AND 90ᵀᴴ ANNIVERSARY PATCHES

This year has been a very exciting year for patch collecting. With the Boy Scouts of America celebrating its 90th anniversary and everyone caught up in millennium fever, many Special Activity Patches (SAPs) were designed and issued. In all, we collected forty-four millennium SAPs, with Green Mountain, Southeast Louisiana, and Southern New Jersey being camera shy. We also collected thirty-eight 90th anniversary SAPs, but Golden Empire, Gulf Coast (Texas), Los Angeles Area, and Robert E. Lee patches were unavailable. Others are planned for later this year.

For those who plan to collect some or all of these patches, be forewarned that many are out-of-stock and others are Friends of Scouting (FOS) patches that may be available but can be expensive.

MILLENNIUM PATCHES

Scout_____ Date _____ Tel_____ E-mail _____
Scout_____ Date _____ Tel_____ E-mail _____

Scout_____ Date _____ Tel_____ E-mail _____
Scout_____ Date _____ Tel_____ E-mail _____

Scout_____ Date _____ Tel_____ E-mail _____
Scout_____ Date _____ Tel_____ E-mail _____

Scout_____ Date _____ Tel_____ E-mail _____
Scout_____ Date _____ Tel_____ E-mail _____

Scout_____ Date _____ Tel_____ E-mail _____
Scout_____ Date _____ Tel_____ E-mail _____

Scout_____ Date _____ Tel_____ E-mail _____
Scout_____ Date _____ Tel_____ E-mail _____

Flint   River

Scout_____ Date _____ Tel_____ E-mail _____
Scout_____ Date _____ Tel_____ E-mail _____

Scout_____ Date _____ Tel_____ E-mail _____
Scout_____ Date _____ Tel_____ E-mail _____

Greater   Alabama

Scout_____ Date _____ Tel_____ E-mail _____
Scout_____ Date _____ Tel_____ E-mail _____

Scout_____ Date _____ Tel_____ E-mail _____
Scout_____ Date _____ Tel_____ E-mail _____

MILLENNIUM PATCHES

Scout_____ Date _____ Tel_____ E-mail _____
Scout_____ Date _____ Tel_____ E-mail _____

Scout_____ Date _____ Tel_____ E-mail _____
Scout_____ Date _____ Tel_____ E-mail _____

Scout_____ Date _____ Tel_____ E-mail _____
Scout_____ Date _____ Tel_____ E-mail _____

Scout_____ Date _____ Tel_____ E-mail _____
Scout_____ Date _____ Tel_____ E-mail _____

National   Capital

Scout_____ Date _____ Tel_____ E-mail _____
Scout_____ Date _____ Tel_____ E-mail _____

Scout_____ Date _____ Tel_____ E-mail _____
Scout_____ Date _____ Tel_____ E-mail _____

Scout_____ Date _____ Tel_____ E-mail _____
Scout_____ Date _____ Tel_____ E-mail _____

Scout_____ Date _____ Tel_____ E-mail _____
Scout_____ Date _____ Tel_____ E-mail _____

Suwannee   River

Scout_____ Date _____ Tel_____ E-mail _____
Scout_____ Date _____ Tel_____ E-mail _____

Scout_____ Date _____ Tel_____ E-mail _____
Scout_____ Date _____ Tel_____ E-mail _____

Scout_____ Date _____ Tel_____ E-mail _____
Scout_____ Date _____ Tel_____ E-mail _____

Scout_____ Date _____ Tel_____ E-mail _____
Scout_____ Date _____ Tel_____ E-mail _____

Scout_____ Date _____ Tel_____ E-mail _____
Scout_____ Date _____ Tel_____ E-mail _____

Scout_____ Date _____ Tel_____ E-mail _____
Scout_____ Date _____ Tel_____ E-mail _____

Scout_____ Date _____ Tel_____ E-mail _____
Scout_____ Date _____ Tel_____ E-mail _____

Scout_____ Date _____ Tel_____ E-mail _____
Scout_____ Date _____ Tel_____ E-mail _____

Scout_____ Date _____ Tel_____ E-mail _____
Scout_____ Date _____ Tel_____ E-mail _____

Scout_____ Date _____ Tel_____ E-mail _____
Scout_____ Date _____ Tel_____ E-mail _____

Scout_____ Date _____ Tel_____ E-mail _____
Scout_____ Date _____ Tel_____ E-mail _____

Scout_____ Date _____ Tel_____ E-mail _____
Scout_____ Date _____ Tel_____ E-mail _____

Scout_____ Date _____ Tel_____ E-mail _____
Scout_____ Date _____ Tel_____ E-mail _____

Scout_____ Date _____ Tel_____ E-mail _____
Scout_____ Date _____ Tel_____ E-mail _____

Scout_____ Date _____ Tel_____ E-mail _____
Scout_____ Date _____ Tel_____ E-mail _____

Scout_____ Date _____ Tel_____ E-mail _____
Scout_____ Date _____ Tel_____ E-mail _____

Scout_____ Date _____ Tel_____ E-mail _____
Scout_____ Date _____ Tel_____ E-mail _____

Scout_____ Date _____ Tel_____ E-mail _____
Scout_____ Date _____ Tel_____ E-mail _____

Scout_____ Date _____ Tel_____ E-mail _____
Scout_____ Date _____ Tel_____ E-mail _____

Scout_____ Date _____ Tel_____ E-mail _____
Scout_____ Date _____ Tel_____ E-mail _____

Scout_____ Date _____ Tel_____ E-mail _____
Scout_____ Date _____ Tel_____ E-mail _____

Scout_____ Date _____ Tel_____ E-mail _____
Scout_____ Date _____ Tel_____ E-mail _____

Scout_____ Date _____ Tel_____ E-mail _____
Scout_____ Date _____ Tel_____ E-mail _____

ABOUT THE AUTHORS

S & E PUBLISHING Pomona, NY **Type** R **Issue** 9/98 **Lodge** Delman
Description: This patch was designed by Steve and Elisa Delman (S & E) and represents
some of the family's hobbies and interests. The patch itself represents the family's 14
years of involvement with Boy Scouts of America. The royal blue sky was chosen to
symbolize Steve's fascination with all things astronomical. Also in this vein, a comet (a
cosmic snowball) streaks across the sky, a solar eclipse radiates its corona, and the constellation of Cassiopeia brightens the night. Cassiopeia is a northern constellation located
near the celestial pole. It is made up of five stars, which form the letter W. The five stars
represent the five shining stars in the Delman's lives, their children. The constellation is
named for the mythological Ethiopian queen Cassiopeia, the mother of Andromeda. Legend has it that upon the queen's death she was changed into the constellation. According
to Greek mythology, Cassiopeia boasted that she was more beautiful than the sea nymphs
(Nereids). The nymphs complained to the god of the sea, Poseidon, who proceeded to
send a sea monster to wreak havoc upon the land. Poseidon demanded that Cassiopeia's
daughter, Andromeda, be sacrificed to the monster as punishment for her mother's vanity.
The great mortal hero, Perseus, came to the rescue by saving Princess Andromeda and
making her his wife. The winter sky features the constellation named for him. It is posi-
tioned near the constellations of Cassiopeia and Andromeda. Within Andromeda is the
Andromeda Galaxy, the Earth's nearest spiral galaxy, 2.2 million light-years away. It is
the most distant object that can be seen with the naked eye. Steve and Elisa have traveled
to such places as Mexico, the Netherlands Antillies, and Toledo, Ohio to catch a glimpse
of a solar eclipse. A solar eclipse occurs when the sun is partially or totally obscured by
the moon, causing a shadow to be cast upon the earth. Such features as the corona (the
outer solar atmosphere of the sun), Baily's Beads (a phenomenon manifested as brilliant
points of light caused by the irregularities of the edge of the disk of the moon), the Diamond Ring, shadow bands, and prominences can all be seen when viewing a total eclipse
of the sun. The family has also spent time traveling in their recreational vehicle exploring
our magnificent nation from coast to coast. The patch's orange and red area with the cactus symbolizes America's west, while the green trees and rolling hills are reminiscent of
America's east. A soaring eagle is pictured signifying son Gregg and his rank as an Eagle
Scout. Kim, one of the Delman's daughters and the book's official patch scanner, is signi-
fied by the icon for Capricorn (the ram), which is seen in the lower left corner of the
patch. The moose illustrates Elisa's enchantment with the majestic animals. Whether
Bullwinkle, the moose of Yellowstone National Park, Alaska, or New England, or one of
her numerous knickknacks and stuffed-toy moose she loves them all. Lastly, the bright
gold book stands for The Boy Scout Council Shoulder Patch Guide and the other patch
books that are in the works.
Scout_____ Date _____ Tel_____ E-mail _____

PATCH AND COUNCIL UPDATES
NEW CSP DESIGNS

Blue Mountain
Bucks County
Calumet
Central Florida
Central New Jersey
Cherokee Area-TN
Circle Ten
Clinton Valley
Colonial Virginia
Dan Beard
Erie Shores
Far East
Four Lakes

French Creek
Gateway Area
Golden Empire
Grand Teton
Greater Yosemite
Hiawatha Seaway
Indian Waters
Indianhead
Long Beach Area
Long Horn
Longs Peak
Middle Tennessee
Mohegan

Mountaineer
Northeast Illinois
Northern Lights
Northern New Jersey
Oregon Trail
Patriots' Path
Quivara
San Gabriel Valley
Sinnissippi
Southeast Louisiana
Southern New Jersey
Tidewater
Transatlantic

DESIGN VARIATIONS[1]

Black Hills
Blackhawk
Finger Lakes
Five Rivers
General Herkimer

Great Rivers
Great Salt Lake
Greater Niagara Frontier
Hudson Valley
Keystone Area

Ozark Trails
Rainbow
Rio Grande
Shawnee Trails
Southeast Wisconsin
Trails West

RETIRED CSPs

Bay Lakes
Bergen
Buffalo Trail
California Inland Empire
George Washington
Greater Lowell
Greater NY Eagle

Hiawatha
Moraine Trails
Morris-Sussex
Muskingum Valley
New Orleans Area
Panama Canal
Pine Tree

Prairie Gold Area
Saudi Arabia
Seaway Valley
Thomas Edison
Toledo Area
Watchung
Westchester-Putnam

COUNCIL MERGERS AND NEW NAMES

COUNCIL NAME	MERGED WITH	NEW COUNCIL'S NAME
Bergen	Name change only	Northern New Jersey
George Washington	Thomas Edison	Central New Jersey
Great Salt Plains[2]	Will Rogers	Cimarron Area
Greater Lowell	Yankee Clipper	Yankee Clipper
Hiawatha	Seaway Valley	Hiawatha Seaway
Mid-America	Prairie Gold Area	Mid-America
Morris-Sussex	Watchung	Patriots' Path
New Orleans Area	Name change only	Southeast Louisiana
Prairie Gold Area	Mid-America	Mid-America
Seaway Valley	Hiawatha	Hiawatha Seaway
Thomas Edison	George Washington	Central New Jersey
Toledo Area	Name change only	Erie Shores
Watchung	Morris-Sussex	Patriots' Path
Will Rogers[2]	Great Salt Plains	Cimarron Area
Yankee Clipper	Greater Lowell	Yankee Clipper

[1] Small design or color changes
[2] Merger occurred June 12, 2000, and was too late to be included in this update.

ASK THE AUTHORS

Q. *When did Council Shoulder Patch collecting first begin?*
A. It all started on April 17, 1970 when the National Insignia and Uniform Committee with approval of the National Executive Committee issued a letter establishing new Council Insignia designs. These new Insignia designs forever changed the simple "red and white" strips called Community and State Council Strips replacing them with the more colorful and interesting Council Shoulder Patches.

Q. *What is CSP collecting?*
A. To some, it is trying to collect all of their own Council's CSPs—from the first issued to the current one. To others, it is trying to collect the CSPs from all Councils, or maybe just from the Councils in their state or region.

Q. *How many CSPs are there?*
A. We do not know the exact total, but our best guess is over 4,000.

Q. *How many different CSP shapes are there?*
A. There are three different shapes. Examples of the three shapes are exemplified by the following Councils: Alabama-Florida, page 1; Black Warrior, page 1; and South Florida, page 14.

Q. *How many CSPs does a Council have?*
A. It varies. Some Councils have issued only one, while others issue a CSP each year. Special Activity Patches (SAPs), which are the same shape as CSPs, are made to commemorate special events and activities, but are not considered a CSP.

Q. *Are older CSPs available?*
A. Yes. Keep in mind, the older a patch is, the rarer and more expensive it will be. We must caution you that occasionally rare, expensive patches have been duplicated and these "fakes" have been sold as originals.

Q. *What is the best way to obtain current CSPs?*
A. There are many ways to obtain CSPs. The ideal way to collect CSPs is to swap yours with other Scouts. You can meet swappers at Patch (Trade)-O-Rees and larger Scouting events such as the National Jamboree. Another way to swap is to join the American Scout Traders Association, Inc. (ASTA). This group of Scouts and Scouters collect many types of Scouting memorabilia (see page 98).

You can also purchase CSPs. If the Type is "U," you can call BSA National Supply and order them. The phone number is 1-800-323-0732. If the CSP Type is "N" or "R," call or write the Council. Almost every Council will accept a phone order with a major credit card. Council phone numbers can be found in the Council Information Reference on pages 99-108.

Q. *Are there any Internet Scouting resources?*
A. Yes. Visit S & E Publishing at **www.scoutpatch.com** and we will provide links to any other Scouting sites and Councils. The Boy Scouts of America's website can be found at **www.bsa.scouting.org**. The BSA's Supply Division internet ordering site is **www.scoutstuff.org**.

Q. *What books do you recommend?*
A. Some of the commonly used books can be found on page 98.

SCOUT MUSEUMS

The following is a list of some of the Boy Scout Museums you can visit throughout the U.S. Please note museums with an (*) are seasonal or by appointment only, so please write or phone before visiting. Visit our website to learn more about these museums.

ARIZONA
Scout Museum of Southern
  Arizona*
1937 East Blacklidge Drive
Tucson, AZ 85719
520-326-7669

COLORADO
Koshare Indian Museum
115 West 18th Street
La Junta, CO 81050
719-384-4411 or
800-693-kiva

FLORIDA
Boy Scout Museum
Casements Culture Center
25 Riverside Drive
Ormand Beach, FL 32176
904-676-3216

ILLINOIS
Ottowa Scout Museum
1100 Canal Street
Ottawa, IL 61350
815-431-9353

KANSAS
Central States Scout
  Museum
815 Broadway
Larned, KS 67550
316-285-8938 or 6427

KENTUCKY
National Scout Museum
Boy Scouts of America
1 Murray Street
Murray, KY 42071-3316
800-303-3047

MICHIGAN
Owaisippe Museum
Chicago Council Camp
9900 Russell Road
Twin Lakes, MI 49457
Summers only
231-894-4061

MICHIGAN
Frances Scout Museum*
12417 State Road
Nunica, MI 49448
616-842-2178

Washington Historical
  Scouting Museum*
56550 Stonewyck Drive
Shelby Twp, MI 48316
810-781-4703

MINNESOTA
North Star Scouting
  Memorabilia
130 North 3rd Avenue, South
Saint Paul, MN 55075
651-771-9066

MISSISSIPPI
L.O. Crosby Jr. Visitor
  Center
Scout Camp Tiak, BSA
Wiggins, MS 39577
601-928-9672

NEW HAMPSHIRE
Lawrence Lee Scouting
  Museum
Camp Carpenter, BSA
RFD #6 P.O. Box 1121
Manchester, NH 03105
603-669-8919

NEW MEXICO
Philmont Museum/Seton
  Memorial Library
Philmont Scout Ranch
Cimarron, NM 87714
505-376-2281

NEW YORK
Trailside Museum
Dan Beard Exhibit
Bear Mountain State Park
Bear Mountain, NY 10911
845-786-2701

NEW YORK
Hiawatha Council Scout
  Museum*
Camp Woodlands
491 Kibbie Lake Road
Constantia, NY 13044
315-623-9316

NORTH CAROLINA
Lone Scout Museum
Camp John J. Barnhardt
42830 Cannon Road
New London, NC 28127
704-422-3025

OHIO
Nathan L. Dauby Scout
  Museum
Greater Cleveland Council
BSA Scout Center
East 22nd Street at Woodlawn
Cleveland, OH 44115
216-861-6060

PENNSYLVANIA
World of Scouting Museum
P.O. Box 2226
Valley Forge, PA 19482
610-783-5311

VIRGINIA
Shenandoah Area Council
  Museum
107 Youth Development
  Court
Winchester, VA 22602-2425
540-662-2551

WISCONSIN
Heritage Scout Museum
Milwaukee County Council
330 South 84th Street
Milwaukee, WI 53214
414-774-1776

SOURCES FOR FURTHER INFORMATION

To those interested in learning more about patch collecting, below is a short list of some of the most commonly used books and Internet Scouting resources. This is intended to be a starting point, many other books and resources are available. Check our website at www.scoutpatch.com for additional information and updates.

American Scout Traders Association, Inc, P.O. Box 210013, San Francisco, CA 94121-0013. Website http://scouter.org/asta

Boy Scouts of America, 972-580-2000, website www.bsa.scouting.org

Boy Scouts of America National Supply, 800-323-0732, www.scoutstuff.org

COUNCIL SHOULDER PATCH SOURCES

D. Franck, D. Hook, J. Ellis & T. Jones. *Aid to Collecting Selected Council Shoulder Patches.* Garland, Texas (Phone: 972-530-7863)

Illinois Traders Association. *Guide to Collecting Selected Council Shoulder Patches.* Norwell, Massachusetts (Phone: 617-659-2115)

ORDER OF THE ARROW SOURCES

Walika Publishing Company. *Arapaho: A History of the Order of the Arrow Through Insignia.* Universal City, California. (www.walika.com/arapaho.htm)

J. Morley, J. Pleasants, B. Topkis, B. Shelley, et al *The Blue Book: Standard Order of the Arrow Insignia Catalog.* 2d Ed. American Scouting Historical Society Park City, Utah 1998. (Phone: 919-742-2967)

BIBLIOGRAPHY

AAA Map'n'Go® 2.0. for *Windows*® Computer Software. DeLorme, 1996. IBM PC CD-Rom.

Botkin, B. A., ed. *A Treasury of American Folklore.* New York: Bantam Books, Inc., 1981.

Francis, Lee. *Native Time.* New York: St. Martin's Press, 1996.

Johansen, Bruce E., and Donald A. Grinde, Jr. *The Encyclopedia of Native American Biography.* New York: Henry Holt and Company, 1997.

Microsoft® *Encarta 2000 Encyclopedia Deluxe.* Computer software. Microsoft Corporation, 1993-2000. IBM PC CD-Rom.

®*TourBook* 21 Catalogs. Heathrow, Fla.: American Automobile Association, 1995-2000.

Waldman, Carl. *Encyclopedia of Native American Tribes.* New York: Facts On File, Inc., 1988.

COUNCIL INFORMATION REFERENCE

Abraham Lincoln
1911 West Monroe Road
Springfield, IL 62704-1596
Phone: 217-546-5570
no website
Adirondack
1 Sesame Street
Plattsburgh, NY 12901-0238
Phone: 518-561-0360
no website
Alabama-Florida
6801 West Main Street
Dothan, AL 36301
Phone: 334-793-7882
website under construction
Alameda
1714 Everett Street
Alameda, CA 94501-0222
Phone: 510-522-2772
www.bsa-alameda.org
Alamo Area
2226 NW Military Highway
San Antonio, TX 78213
Phone: 210-341-8611
www.alamoarea-boyscouts.org
Alapaha Area
1841 Norman Drive
Valdosta, GA 31603
Phone: 912-242-2331
no website
Allegheny Highlands
50 Hough Hill Road
Falconer, NY 14733
Phone: 716-665-2697
home.penn.com/ahcbsa
Allohak
1340 Juliana Street
Parkersburg, WV 26101
Phone: 304-422-4507
www.allohak.org
Aloha
42 Puiwa Road
Honolulu, HI 96808
Phone: 808-595-6366
www.boyscoutshawaii.org
Andrew Jackson
855 Riverside Drive
Jackson, MS 39202-1199
Phone: 601-948-6111
no website
Annawon
219 Winthrop Street
Tauton, MA 02780
Phone: 508-824-4164
No website

Anthony Wayne Area
3635 Portage Boulevard
Fort Wayne, IN 46802
Phone: 219-432-9593
www.bsaawac.org
Arbuckle Area
411 State Highway 142 West
Ardmore, OK 73403-0309
Phone: 580-223-0831
www.arbucklebsa.org
Atlanta Area
100 Edgewood Ave, N.E.
Atlanta, GA 30303-3068
Phone: 404-577-4810
No website
Attakapas
1545 Jackson Street
Alexandria, LA 71301-6934
Phone: 318-443-0482
www.attakapas.org
Baden Powell
113 South Jensen Street
Vestal, NY 13850
Phone: 607-729-9161
www.ithaca.ny.us/Orgs/
    Scouts/baden.html
Baltimore Area
701 Wyman Park Drive
Baltimore, MD 21211-2805
Phone: 410-338-1700
www.baltimorebsa.org
Bay Area
3020 53rd Street
Galveston, TX 77551
Phone: 409-744-5207
www.bacbsa.org
Bay Lakes
1650 Midway Road
Menasha, WI 54952-0516
Phone: 920-734-5705
www.baylakesbsa.org
Black Hills Area
144 North Street
Rapid City, SD 57701
Phone: 605-342-2824
www.bsa-bhac.org
Black Swamp Area
2100 Broad Avenue
Findlay, OH 45840-2748
Phone: 419-422-4356
No web site
Black Warrior
2700 River Road, NE
Tuscaloosa, AL 35403-3088
Phone: 205-554-1680
bwcbsa.tusc.net

Blackhawk Area
1800 7th Avenue
Rockford, IL 61104
Phone: 815-397-0210
No website
Blue Grass
415 North Broadway
Lexington, KY 40508-1301
Phone: 859-231-7811
www.bgbsa.org
Blue Mountain
8478 West Gage Boulevard
Kennewick, WA 99336-1075
Phone: 509-735-7306
No website
Blue Ridge
2 Ridgeway Avenue
Greenville, SC 29607
Phone: 864-233-8363
No website
Blue Ridge Mountains
2131 Valley View Boulevard
Roanoke, VA 24019-0606
Phone: 540-265-0656
www.bsa-brmc.org
Blue Water
901 Huron Avenue
Port Huron, MI 48060
Phone: 810-982-9529
www.bwcbsa.com
Boston Minuteman
199 State Street, 3rd Floor
Boston, MA 02130-2796
Phone: 617-723-0007
www.bsaboston.org
Boulder Dam Area
1135 University Road
Las Vegas, NV 89119-6605
Phone: 702-736-4366
www.bdacbsa.org
Boys Scouts Of America
1325 West Walnut Hill Lane
Irving, TX 75015
Phone: 972-580-2000
www.bsa.scouting.org
BSA Supply Division
National Distribution Center
P.O. Box 7143
Charlotte, NC 28241-7143
Phone: 800-323-0732
www.scoutstuff.org
Buckeye
2301 13th Street, N.W.
Canton, OH 44708-3157
Phone: 330-580-4272
No web site

COUNCIL INFORMATION REFERENCE

Bucks County
1 Scout Way
Doylestown, PA 18901
Phone: 215-348-9436
www.voicenet.com/~campock

Buckskin
2829 Kanawha Blvd, East
Charleston, WV 25311-1727
Phone: 304-340-3663
No website

Bucktail
209 First Street
Du Bois, PA 15801-3007
Phone: 814-371-5650
home.penn.com/bucktail

Buffalo Trace
1050 Bayard Park Drive
Evansville, IN 47731-3245
Phone: 812-423-5246
members.sigecom.net/bsa156

Buffalo Trail
1101 West Texas Avenue
Midland, TX 79701
Phone: 915-570-7601
No website

Burlington County
693 Rancocas Road
Rancocas, NJ 08060
Phone: 609-261-5850
No website

Caddo Area
24 Lynwood Drive
Texarkana, TX 75505-5807
Phone: 903-793-2179
No website

Calcasieu Area
304 South Ryan Street
Lake Charles, LA 70601
Phone: 337-436-3376
No website

California Inland Empire
1230 Indiana Court
Redlands, CA 92374
Phone: 909-793-2463
www.bsa-ciec.org

Calumet
8751 Calumet Avenue
Munster, IN 46321
Phone: 708-474-6212
www.jorsm.com/calcouncil

Cambridge
2326 Massachusetts Avenue
Cambridge, MA 02140
Phone: 617-547-2760
cambridge229.tripod.com

Cape Cod & the Islands
247 Willow Street
Yarmouth Port, MA 02675
Phone: 508-362-4322
www.scoutscapecod.org

Cape Fear
110 Longstreet Drive
Wilmington, NC 28412
Phone: 910-395-1100
No website

Capitol Area
7540 Ed Bluestein Boulevard
Austin, TX 78723-2399
Phone: 512-926-6363
www.bsa-austin.org

Cascade Pacific
2145 Naito Parkway
Portland, OR 97201-5197
Phone: 503-226-3423
www.cpcbsa.org

Catalina
5049 East Broadway
Tucson, AZ 85711-3636
Phone: 520-750-0385
www.catalinacouncil.org

Cayuga County
63 Genesee Street
Auburn, NY 13021-3600
Phone: 315-252-9579
No website

Central Florida
1951 S. Orange Blossom Trail
Apopka, FL 32703-7747
Phone: 407-889-4403
www.cfcbsa.org

Central Georgia
2465 Hillcrest Avenue
Macon, GA 31204-4039
Phone: 912-743-9386
No website

Central Minnesota
1701 9th Avenue North
St. Cloud, MN 56303-1412
Phone: 320-251-3930
No website

Central New Jersey
4315 U.S. Highway 1 South
Monmouth Junction, NJ 08852
Phone: 609-419-1600
www.gwc.org

Central North Carolina
32252 Highway 24-27
Albermarle, NC 28001
Phone: 704-982-0141
www.centralncbsa.com

Central Wyoming
3939 Casper Mountain Road
Casper, WY 82602-1506
Phone: 307-234-7329
www.wyoscouts.org

Chattahoocee
1710 Buena Vista Road
Columbus, GA 31906
Phone: 706-327-2634
No Web Site

Cherokee Area - OK
121 S.E. Adams Boulevard
Bartlesville, OK 74003-4925
Phone: 918-336-9170
www.cherokeescouter.org

Cherokee Area - TN
6031 Lee Highway
Chattanooga, TN 37421-2930
Phone: 423-892-8323
www.chattanooga.net/boyscouts

Chester County
504 South Concord Road
West Chester, PA 19382
Phone: 610-696-2900
www.cccbsa.org

Chicago Area
1218 West Adams
Chicago, IL 60607-2802
Phone: 312-421-8800
www.chicagobsa.org

Chickasaw
171 South Hollywood Street
Memphis, TN 38112-4802
Phone: 901-327-4193
No website

Chief Cornplanter
316 Fourth Avenue
Warren, PA 16365-2320
Phone: 814-723-6700
users.penn.com/~cccbsa

Chief Okemos
4000 West Michigan
Lansing, MI 48917-2807
Phone: 517-321-7278
No website

Chief Seattle
3120 Rainier Avenue
Seattle, WA 98144-9758
Phone: 206-725-5200
www.seattlebsa.org

Chippewa Valley
710 South Hastings Way
Eau Claire, WI 54701
Phone: 715-832-6671
No website

Chisholm Trail
1208 North 5th Street
Abilene, TX 79601-5020
Phone: 915-677-2688
www.chisholm-trail-bsa.org

Choctaw Area
2401 9th Street
Meridian, MS 39301
Phone: 601-693-6757
No Web Site

Circle Ten
8605 Harry Hines Boulevard
Dallas, TX 75235-0726
Phone: 214-351-1010
www.circle10.org

Clinton Valley
1100 County Center Drive
Waterford, MI 48328
Phone: 248-338-0035
www.cvc-bsa.org

Coastal Carolina
1025 Sam Rittenberg Blvd.
Charleston, SC 29407-3441
Phone: 843-763-0305
No website

Coastal Empire
11900 Abercorn Extension
Savannah, GA 31419
Phone: 912-927-7272
www.bsasavannah.org

Colonial Virginia
11725 Jefferson Avenue
Newport News, VA 23606
Phone: 757-595-3356
www.cvcboyscouts.org

Columbia-Montour
212 West 5th Street
Bloomsburg, PA 17815-2133
Phone: 570-784-2700
www.sunlink.net/
    ~tgusl/colmon.htm

Comanche Trail
602 East Adams Street
Brownwood, TX 76804-1086
Phone: 915-646-0616
www.bwoodtx.com/bsa

Concho Valley
104 West River Drive
San Angelo, TX 76902-1584
Phone: 915-655-7107
home1.gte.net/bsa741

Connecticut Rivers
60 Darlin Street
East Hartford, CT 06128
Phone: 860-289-6669
www.ctrivers.org

Connecticut Yankee
60 Wellinton Road
Milford, CT 06460
Phone: 203-876-6868
www.ctyankee.org

Conquistador
2603 North Aspen Avenue
Roswell, NM 88201
Phone: 505-622-3461
www.conquistador-bsa.org

Cornhusker
201 Oakcreek Drive
Lincoln, NE 68528
Phone: 402-476-8846
www.cornhuskercouncil.org

Coronado Area
644 South Ohio
Salina, KS 67401
Phone: 785-827-4461
www.salhelp.org/boyscouts

Cradle of Liberty
22nd & Winter Streets
Philadelphia, PA 19103-1085
Phone: 215-988-9811
www.colbsa.org

Crater Lake
3039 Hanley Road
Central Point, OR 97502
Phone: 541-664-1444
www.craterlakecouncil.org

Crossroads of America
1900 North Meridian Street
Indianapolis, IN 46206-1966
Phone: 317-925-1900
www.crossroadsbsa.org

Dan Beard
2331 Victory Parkway
Cincinnati, OH 45206-2803
Phone: 513-961-2336
www.danbeard.org

Daniel Boone
64 W. T. Weaver Boulevard
Asheville, NC 28814-8010
Phone: 828-254-6189
www.main.nc.us/
    DanielBooneCouncil

Daniel Webster
571 Holt Avenue
Manchester, NH 03109
Phone: 603-625-6431
www.dwcbsa.org

De Soto Area
118 West Peach Street
El Dorado, AR 71730
Phone: 870-863-5166
No website

Del-Mar-Va
801 Washington Street
Wilmington, DE 19801-1597
Phone: 302-622-3300
www.delmarvacouncil.com

Denver Area
2901 West 19th Avenue
Denver, CO 80204-1786
Phone: 303-455-5522
www.denverareacouncil.com

Des Plaines Valley
811 West Hillgrove Avenue
La Grange, IL 60525-5822
Phone: 708-354-1111
www.bsa-dpvc.org

Desert Pacific
1207 Upas Street
San Diego, CA 92103
Phone: 619-298-6121
www.boyscoutsofsocal.com

Detroit Area
1776 West Warren Avenue
Detroit, MI 48208
Phone: 313-897-1965
www.dacbsa.org

Direct Service, BSA
1325 Walnut Hill Lane
Irving, TX 77015
Phone: 972-580-2406
www.directservicecouncil.org

East Carolina
313 Boy Scout Boulevard
Kinston, NC 28503-1698
Phone: 252-522-1521
No website

East Texas Area
1331 East Fifth Street
Tyler, TX 75701-3427
Phone: 903-597-7201
No website

Eastern Arkansas Area
1000 S. Caraway Road
#112 A-B
Jonesboro, AR 72401-0146
Phone: 870-932-3871
www.eaac.org

Erie Shores
1 Stranahan Square, Ste 226
Toledo, OH 43604
Phone: 419-241-7293
www.toledobsa.com

Evangeline Area
2266 South College Road, Ext
Lafayette, LA 70598-0115
Phone: 337-235-8552
No website

Far East, MCB Camp Foster
APO AP 96343
Phone: 011-81-3117-63-7497
www.geocities.com/Tokyo/
Ginza/3451

Finger Lakes
3685 Pre-Emption Road
Geneva, NY 14456-9138
Phone: 315-789-1166
www2.grady.com/
bsafingerlakes/index.html

Five Rivers
3300 Chambers Road, South
Horseheads, NY 14844-5190
Phone: 607-796-0699
www.fiverivers.org

Flint River
1361 Zebulon Road
Griffin, GA 30224-0173
Phone: 770-227-4556
www.thunderbsa.org

Florida Sea Base
73800 Overseas Highway
Islamorada, FL 33036
Phone: 305-664-4173
www.bsaseabase.org

Four Lakes
34 Schroeder Court
Madison, WI 53711-2525
Phone: 608-273-1005
www.flcbsa.org

French Creek
1815 Robison Road West
Erie, PA 16509-4905
Phone: 814-868-5571
www.usachoice.com/fccbsa

Gamehaven
1124 11-1/2 Street, SE
Rochester, MN 55904-5097
Phone: 507-287-1410
www.gamehavencouncil.org

Gateway Area
2600 Quarry Road
La Crosse, WI 54601-3997
Phone: 608-784-4040
No website

General Herkimer
427 North Main
Herkimer, NY 13357
Phone: 315-866-1540
newport.ntcnet.com/~bsa400

Georgia-Carolina
1804 Gordon Highway
Augusta, GA 30904-5637
Phone: 706-733-5277
www.gacacouncil.org

Gerald R. Ford
3213 Walker Avenue, NW
Grand Rapids, MI 49544
Phone: 616-785-2662
www.grfccouncilbsa.org

Golden Empire
251 Commerce Circle
Sacramento, CA 95815
Phone: 916-929-1417
www.gec-bsa.org

Golden Spread
401 Tascosa Road
Amarillo, TX 79124
Phone: 806-358-6500
www.goldenspread.org

Grand Canyon
2969 North Greenfield Road
Phoenix, AZ 85016-7715
Phone: 602-955-7747
www.grandcanyonbsa.org

Grand Columbia
2331 South 18th Street
Union Gap, WA 98903
Phone: 509-453-4795
No website

Grand Teton
574 4th Street
Idaho Falls, ID 83401
Phone: 208-522-5155
No website

Great Rivers
1203 Fay Street
Columbia, MO 65205
Phone: 573-449-2561
www.bsa-grc.org

Great Salt Lake
525 Foothill Boulevard
Salt Lake City, UT 84113
Phone: 801-582-3663
www.gslc-bsa.org

Great Salt Plains
317 North Grand
Enid, OK 73702-3146
Phone: 580-234-3652
www.enid.com/gspc

Great Sauk Trail
1979 Huron Parkway
Ann Arbor, MI 48104-4199
Phone: 734-971-7100
No website

Great Smoky Mountain
6440 Papermill Road, NW
Knoxville, TN 37919
Phone: 423-588-6514
www.bsa-gsmc.org

Great Southwest
5841 Office Boulevard., NE
Albuquerque, NM 87109
Phone: 505-345-8603
No website

Great Trail
1601 South Main Street
Akron, OH 44309
Phone: 330-773-0415
No website

Great Trails
88 Old Windsor Road
Dalton, MA 01226-1398
Phone: 413-684-3542
No website

Greater Alabama
516 Liberty Parkway
Birmingham, AL 35243-0307
Phone: 205-970-0251
www.bsagreateralabama.org

Greater Cleveland
2241 Woodland Avenue
Cleveland, OH 44115
Phone: 216-861-6060
www.gccbsa.org

Greater New York
350 Fifth Avenue, 4th Floor
New York, NY 10018-0199
Phone: 212-242-1100
www.bsa-gnyc.org

Greater Niagara Frontier
401 Maryvale Drive
Buffalo, NY 14225-2691
Phone: 716-891-4073
www.gnfc-bsa.org

Greater Pittsburgh
Flag Plaza
1275 Bedford Avenue
Pittsburgh, PA 15219-3699
Phone: 412-471-2927
www.gpc-bsa.org

Greater St. Louis Area
4568 West Pine Boulevard
St. Louis, MO 63108-2193
Phone: 314-361-0600
www.stlbsa.org

Greater Western Reserve
4390 Enterprise Drive
Warren, OH 44481
Phone: Phone: 330-898-8474
www.bsa-gwrc.org

Greater Yosemite Area
4031 Technology Drive
Modesto, CA 95356
Phone: Phone: 209-545-6320
www.inreach.com/scouter/gyc

Green Mountain
Route 2
Waterbury, VT 05676
Phone: 802-244-5189
hometown.aol.com/gmcbsa

Greenwich
63 Mason Street
Greenwich, CT 06830
Phone: 203-869-8424
No website

Gulf Coast- FL
9440 University Parkway
Pensacola, FL 32514-5434
Phone: 850-476-6336
No website

Gulf Coast -TX
700 Everhart Terrace
Building A
Corpus Cristi, TX 78411
Phone: 361-814-4300
www.gulfcc.org

Gulf Ridge
4410 Boy Scout Boulevard
Tampa, FL 33607-5704
Phone: 813-872-2691
www.boyscouting.com

Gulf Stream
8335 North Military Trail
Palm Beach Gardens, FL 33410
Phone: 561-694-8585
No website

Hawk Mountain
4901 Pottsville Pike
Reading, PA 19605-9713
Phone: 610-926-3406
www.epix.net/~hawkmtn

Hawkeye Area
320 Collins Road, N.E.
Cedar Rapids, IA 52402
Phone: 319-393-8426
www.hawkeyebsa.org

Heart O'Texas
300 Lake Air Drive
Waco, TX 76710
Phone: 254-772-8932
www.hotboyscouts.org

Heart of America
10210 Holmes Road
Kansas City, MO 64131
Phone: 816-942-9333
www.hoac-bsa.org

Heart of Ohio
445 West Longview Avenue
Mansfield, OH 44903
Phone: 419-522-5091
www.bsa-heartofohio.org

Hiawatha Seaway
113 Twin Oaks Drive
Syracuse, NY 13206-1236
Phone: 315-463-0201
www.cnyscouts.org

Hiawathaland
2210 U.S. 41 South
Marquette, MI 49855
Phone: 906-249-1461
www.up.lib.mi.us/
    UPExplore/bsa/home.htm

Hoosier Trails
2307 East Second
Bloomington, IN 47401-5361
Phone: 812-336-6809
No website

Housatonic
326 Derby Avenue
Derby, CT 06418-2083
Phone: 203-734-3329
www.electronicvalley.org/hcba

Hudson Valley
2130 Rt 94-Station Road Square
Salisbury Mills, NY 12577
Phone: 845-497-7337
www.hvcbsa.org

Illowa
4711 North Brady, Suite 200
Davenport, IA 52806
Phone: 319-388-7233
www.illowabsa.org

Indian Nations
3206 South Peoria
Tulsa, OK 74105
Phone: 918-743-6125
www.okscouts.org

Indian Waters
715 Betsy Drive
Columbia, SC 29202-0144
Phone: 803-750-9868
www.iwc-bsa.com

Indianhead
393 Marshall Avenue
St. Paul, MN 55102-1795
Phone: 651-224-1891
www.indianhead.org

Inland Northwest
411 West Boy Scout Way
Spokane, WA 99201-2243
Phone: 509-325-4562
www.inwc-bsa.org

Iroquois Trail
7121 Rochester Road
Lockport, NY 14094
Phone: 716-434-2851
freenet.buffalo.edu/~iroquois

Istrouma Area
9644 Brookline Avenue
Baton Rouge, LA 70896
Phone: 225-926-2697
www.iac-bsa.org

Jayhawk Area
1020 SE Monroe
Topeka, KS 66612
Phone: 785-354-8541
www.jayhawkcouncil.org

Jersey Shore
1518 Ridgeway Road
Toms River, NJ 08755-4072
Phone: 732-349-1037
www.jerseyshore-bsa.org

Juniata Valley
9 Taylor Drive
Reedsville, PA 17084
Phone: 717-667-9236
No website

Katahdin Area
90 Kelley Road
Orono, ME 04473
Phone: 207-866-3528
www.katahdinareabsa.org

Keystone Area
1 Baden-Powell Lane
Mechanicsburg, PA 17055
Phone: 717-766-1591
www.keystonebsa.org

Knox Trail
490 Union Avenue
Framingham, MA 01702
Phone: 508-872-6551
www.keonet.com/public/
    ktc/ktchome.htm

La Salle
1433 Northside Boulevard
South Bend, IN 46615-1298
Phone: 219-289-0337
www.lasallecouncilbsa.org

Lake Huron Area
5001 South Eleven Mile Road
Auburn, MI 48611-0129
Phone: 517-695-5593
www.lhacbsa.org

Land of the Oneidas
1401 Genesee Street
Utica, NY 13501-4399
Phone: 315-735-4437
No website

Last Frontier
3031 N.W. 64th Street
Oklahoma City, OK 73116
Phone: 405-840-1114
www.lastfrontiercouncil.org

COUNCIL INFORMATION REFERENCE

Lincoln Heritage
824 Phillips Lane
Louisville, KY 40209
Phone: 502-361-2624
www.lhcbsa.org

Lincoln Trails
262 West Prairie
Decatur, IL 62523-1221
Phone: 217-429-2326
No website

Long Beach Area
401 East 37th Street
Long Beach, CA 90807-0338
Phone: 562-427-0911
www.longbeachbsa.org

Longhorn
4917 Briarhaven Road
Fort Worth, TX 76109-4498
Phone: 817-738-5491
www.longhorn.org

Longs Peak
2215 23rd Avenue
Greeley, CO 80632-1166
Phone: 970-330-6305
www.longspeakbsa.org

Los Angeles Area
2333 Scout Way
Los Angeles, CA 90026-4995
Phone: 213-413-4400
www.boyscoutsla.org

Los Padres
4000 Modoc Road
Santa Barbara, CA 93110
Phone: 805-967-0105
No website

Marin
225 West End Avenue
San Rafael, CA 94901-2645
Phone: 415-454-1081
www.boyscouts-marin.org

Mason-Dixon
18600 Crestwood Drive
Hagerstown, MD 21742
Phone: 301-739-1211
www.x-press.net/masondixon

Maui County
200 Liholiho Street
Wailuku Maui, HI 96793
Phone: 808-244-3724
www.mauibsa.com

Mecklenburg County
1410 East 7th Street
Charlotte, NC 28204
Phone: 704-333-5471
www.bsa-mcc.org

Miami Valley
4999 Northcutt Place
Dayton, OH 45414-3843
Phone: 937-278-4825
Web under construction

Mid-America
12401 West Maple Road
Omaha, NE 68164-1853
Phone: 402-431-9272
www.mac-bsa.org

Mid-Iowa
1659 East Euclid
Des Moines, IA 50316-3009
Phone: 515-266-2135
www.bsa-ia.org

Middle Tennessee
3414 Hillsboro Road
Nashville, TN 37215-0409
Phone: 615-383-9724
www.mtcbsa.org

Midnight Sun
1400 Gilliam Way
Fairbanks, AK 99701-6044
Phone: 907-452-1976
www.bsa-midnightsun.org

Milwaukee County
330 South 84th Street
Milwaukee, WI 53214-1468
Phone: 414-774-1776
www.mccbsa.org

Minsi Trails
991 Postal Road
Allenton, PA 18002
Phone: 610-264-8551
www.minsitrails.com

Mississippi Valley
2336 Oak Street
Quincy, IL 62301-3240
Phone: 217-224-0204
www.mississippivalleybsa.org

Mobile Area
2587 Government Boulevard
Mobile, AL 36606-1697
Phone: 334-476-4600
www.bsamobile.org

Moby Dick
651 Orchard Street, Suite 107
New Bedford, MA 02740
Phone: 508-993-9978
www.mobydickbsa.org

Mohegan
19 Harvard Street
Worchester, MA 01609
Phone: 508-752-3768
No website

Monmouth
Deal & Monmouth Roads
Oakhurst, NJ 07755-0188
Phone: 732-531-3636
www.monmouthbsa.org

Montana
820 17th Avenue, South
Great Falls, MT 59405-5999
Phone: 406-761-6000
www.mt.net/~bsa-mt

Monterey Bay Area
55 San Joaquin Street
Salinas, CA 93901-2903
Phone: 831-422-5338
www.montereybayarea.com

Moraine Trails
830 Morton Avenue, Extension
Butler, PA 16001-3398
Phone: 724-287-6791
www.morainetrails.org

Mount Baker
1715 - 100 Place SE
Everett, WA 98208
Phone: 425-338-0380
www.mtbaker.org

Mount Diablo Silverado
800 Ellinwood Way
Pleasant Hill, CA 94523
Phone: 925-674-6100
No website

Mountaineer Area
1831 Speedway
Fairmont, WV 26555
Phone: 304-366-3940
www.macbsa.org

Muskingum Valley
734 Moorehead
Zanesville, OH 43702-2036
Phone: 740-453-0571
No website

Narragansett
175 Broad Street
Providence, RI 02903-4081
Phone: 401-351-8700
www.narragansettbsa.org

Nashua Valley
1980 Lunenburg Road
Lancaster, MA 01523
Phone: 978-534-3532
No website

National Capital Area
9190 Rockville Pike
Bethesda, MD 20814-3897
Phone: 301-530-9360
www.boyscouts-ncac.org

Nat'l Boy Scout Museum
1 Murray Street
Murray, KY 42071-3316
Phone: 800-303-3047
www.bsamuseum.org
NeTseO Trails
3787 N.W. Loop 286
Paris, TX 75461-0995
Phone: 903-784-2538
No website
Nevada Area
Ridgeview Shopping Plaza
5150 Mae Anne, Suite 406
Reno, NV 89523-1860
Phone: 775-787-1111
www.scouter.org
North Florida
521 South Edgewood Avenue
Jacksonville, FL 32205
Phone: 904-388-0591
www.nfcbsa.org
Northeast Georgia
148 Boy Scout Trail
Pendergrass, GA 30567
Phone: 706-693-2446
www.nega-bsa.org
Northeast Illinois
2745 Skokie Valley Road
Highland Park, IL 60035
Phone: 847-433-1813
www.neic.org
Northeast Iowa
10395 Military Road
Dubuque, IA 52003
Phone: 319-556-4343
www.scoutiowa.com
Northeastern Pennsylvania
1 Bob Mellow Drive
Mooic, PA 18507
Phone: 570-451-0350
www.nepabsa.org
Northern Lights
301 South 7th Street
Fargo, ND 58103-1884
Phone: 701-293-5011
www.nlcbsa.org
Northern New Jersey
25 Ramapo Valley Road
Oakland, NJ 07436
Phone: 201-791-8000
www.nnjbsa.org
Northern Tier
58791 Moose Lake Road
Ely, MN 55731
Phone: 218-365-4811
www.ntier.org

Northwest Georgia
501 Broad Street
Rome, GA 30161-1422
Phone: 706-235-5545
www.nega-bsa.org
Northwest Suburban
600 North Wheeling Road
Mount Prospect, IL 60056
Phone: 847-824-6880
www.nwsc.org
Northwest Texas
3604 Maplewood Avenue
Wichita Falls, TX 76308
Phone: 940-696-2735
No website
Norwela
3508 Beverly Place
Shreveport, LA 71104
Phone: 318-868-2774
www.norwela.org
Occoneechee
3231 Atlantic Avenue
Raleigh, NC 27629
Phone: 919-872-4884
www.bsa.net/occoneechee
Ohio River Valley
RD1, GC&P Road
Wheeling, WV 26003
Phone: 304-277-2660
No website
Okaw Valley
1801 North 17th Street
Belleville, IL 62226
Phone: 618-234-9111
www.apci.net/~okawbsa
Okefenokee Area
302 Screven Avenue
Waycross, GA 31501
Phone: 912-283-6016
No website
Old Baldy
1047 West Sixth Street
Ontario, CA 91762
Phone: 909-983-4534
www.obcbsa.org
Old Colony
2438 Washington Street
Canton, MA 02021-1123
Phone: 781-828-8360
No website
Old Hickory
6600 Silas Creek Parkway
Winston-Salem, NC 27106
Phone: 336-760-2900
No website

Old North State
1405 Westover Terrace
Greensboro, NC 27429
Phone: 336-378-9166
No website
Orange County
3590 Harbor Gateway North
Costa Mesa, CA 92626-1425
Phone: 714-546-4990
www.ocbsa.org
Ore-Ida
8901 West Franklin Road
Boise, ID 83709-0638
Phone: 208-376-4411
www.oreida-bsa.org
Oregon Trail
2525 Centennial Boulevard
Eugene, OR 97401
Phone: 541-485-4433
No website
Otetiana
474 East Avenue
Rochester, NY 14607-1992
Phone: 716-244-4210
No website
Otschodela
Route 23, Southside
Oneonta, NY 13820-5356
Phone: 607-432-6491
www.otschodela.org
Ouachita Area
102 Chippewa Court
Hot Springs, AR 71902-1234
Phone: 501-623-6601
No website
Ouachita Valley
2405 Oliver Road
Monroe, LA 71201
Phone: 318-325-4634
www.ovcscouting.org
Overland Trails
807 North Boggs
Grand Island, NE 68803
Phone: 308-382-3717
www.overlandtrailscouncil.org
Ozarks Trails
3015 South Kimbrough Avenue
Springfield, MO 65807
Phone: 417-883-1636
www.ozarktrailsbsa.org
Pacific Harbors
4802 South 19th Street
Tacoma, WA 98405
Phone: 253-752-7731
www.pacific-harbors.org

COUNCIL INFORMATION REFERENCE

Pacific Skyline
1305 Middlefield Road
Palo Alto, CA 94301
Phone: 650-327-5900
www.pacsky.org

Palmetto Area
420 South Church Street
Spartanburg, SC 29304
Phone: 864-585-4391
www.palmetto-bsa.org

Patriots Path
1170 Route 22, West
Mountainside, NJ 07092-2810
Phone: 908-654-9191
www.ppbsa.org

Pee Dee Area
702 South Coit Street
Florence, SC 29501
Phone: 843-662-6306
No website

Penn's Woods
664 Tire Hill Road
Tire Hill, PA 15959-0352
Phone: 814-288-0162
www.pwcbsa.org

Pennsylvania Dutch
630 Janet Avenue
Lancaster, PA 17601-4582
Phone: 717-394-4063
No website

Philmont Scout Ranch
Route 1, Box 35
Cimarron, NM 87714
Phone: 505-376-2281
www.philmont.com

Piedmont - CA
10 Highland Way
Piedmont, CA 94611
Phone: 510-547-4493
www.piedmontbsa.org

Piedmont - NC
1222 East Franklin Boulevard
Gastonia, NC 28053-1059
Phone: 704-864-2694
No website

Pikes Peak
525 East Uintah Street
Colorado Springs, CO 80903
Phone: 719-634-1584
bsapikespeak.webstuff.com

Pine Burr Area
6316 U.S. Highway 49
Hattiesburg, MS 39401
Phone: 601-582-2326
No website

Pine Tree
125 Auburn Street
Portland, ME 04103
Phone: 207-797-5252
www.pinetreebsa.org

Pioneer Valley
249 Exchange Street
Chicopee, MA 01013
Phone: 413-594-9196
No website

Pony Express
1704 Buckingham
St. Joseph, MO 64506
Phone: 816-233-1351
www.ponyexpressbsa.org

Potawatomi Area
N12 W24498 Bluemound Road
Waukesha, WI 53187-0528
Phone: 262-544-4881
No website

Potomac
14416 Mc Mullen Highway
Cumberland, MD 21502
Phone: 301-729-1300
No website

Prairielands
3101 Farber Drive
Champaign, IL 61826
Phone: 217-356-7291
No website

Puerto Rico
Los Frailes, Avenue A
Guaynabo, PR 00936
Phone: 787-790-0323
www.geocities.com/
   Yosemite/9920

Pushmataha Area
420 31st Avenue, North
Columbus, MS 39701-1806
Phone: 662-328-7228
No website

Quapaw Area
3220 Cantrell Road
Little Rock, AR 72202-1847
Phone: 501-664-4780
www.quapawbsa.org

Quivira
1555 East Second Street
Wichita, KS 67214
Phone: 316-264-3386
www.quivira.org

Rainbow
2600 North Winterbottom Road
Morris, IL 60450-9440
Phone: 815-942-4450
www.rainbowcouncilbsa.org

Redwood Empire
2240 Professional Drive
Santa Rosa, CA 95403-3005
Phone: 707-546-8137
No website

Rio Grande
6912 West Expressway 83
Harlingen, TX 78552
Phone: 956-423-0250
No website

Rip Van Winkle
75 Pine Street
Kingston, NY 12401
Phone: 845-339-0846
www.rvwbsa.org

Robert E. Lee
4015 Fitzhugh Avenue
Richmond, VA 23230-3935
Phone: 804-355-4306
www.relcbsa.org

Rocky Mountain
411 South Pueblo Boulevard
Pueblo, CO 81005
Phone: 719-561-1220
www.koshare.org/rmc.html

Sagamore
518 North Main Street
Kokomo, IN 46901
Phone: 765-452-8253
www.sagamoresignals.com

Sam Houston Area
1911 Bagby Street
Houston, TX 77052-2786
Phone: 713-659-8111
www.samhoustonbsa.org

Samoset
720 Grant Street
Wausau, WI 54401-4900
Phone: 715-845-2195
www.samosetcouncil.org

San Francisco Bay Area
1001 Davis Street
San Leandro, CA 94577-1514
Phone: 510-577-9000
www.sfbac.org

San Gabriel Valley
3450 East Sierra Madre
   Boulevard
Pasadena, CA 91107
Phone: 626-351-8815
www.sgvcbsa.org

Santa Clara County
970 West Julian Street
San Jose, CA 95126
Phone: 408-280-5088
www.sccc-scouting.org

Santa Fe Trail
1513.5 East Fulton Terrace
Garden City, KS 67846-6165
Phone: 316-275-5162
www.sftcbsa.org

Scenic Trails
2308 U.S. 31 North
Traverse City, MI 49686
Phone: 231-938-2200
www.stcbsa.org

Sequoia
4539 North Brawley
Frenso, CA 93722-3991
Phone: 559-275-0811
www.sequoiacouncilbsa.org

Sequoyah
129 Boone Ridge Drive
Johnson City, TN 37615
Phone: 423-952-6961
No website

Shawnee Trails
301 Leitchfield Road
Owensboro, KY 42303
Phone: 270-684-9272
No website

Shenandoah Area
107 Youth Development Court
Winchester, VA 22602-2425
Phone: 540-662-2551
www.sac-bsa.org

Simon Kenton
1901 East Dublin-Granville
  Road
Columbus, OH 43229-0207
Phone: 614-436-7200
www.skc-bsa.org

Sinnissippi
2300 East Racine Street
Janesville, WI 53545-4340
Phone: 608-756-4669
No website

Sioux
3200 West 49th Street
Sioux Falls, SD 57106
Phone: 605-361-2697
www.siouxbsa.org

Snake River
2988 Falls Avenue; East
Twin Falls, ID 83301
Phone: 208-733-2067
www.snakeriver.org

South Florida
15255 N. W. 82nd Avenue
Miami Lakes, FL 33016
Phone: 305-364-0020
www.sfcbsa.org

South Plains
30 Briercroft Office Park
Lubbock, TX 79412
Phone: 806-747-2631
www.southplainscouncil.org

Southeast Alaska
9220 Lee Smith Drive
Juneau, AK 99801-8018
Phone: 907-789-8440
No website

Southeast Louisiana
4200 South I-10 Service Rd, W
Metairie, LA 70001
Phone: 504-889-0388
www.bsa-selacouncil.org

Southeast Wisconsin
2319 Northwestern Avenue
Racine, WI 53404
Phone: 262-632-1655
www.sewisbsa.com

Southern New Jersey
4468 South Main Road
Millville, NJ 08332-1464
Phone: 856-327-1700
www.snjscouting.org

Southern Sierra
2417 M Street
Bakersfield, CA 93301-2341
Phone: 661-325-9036
www.southernsierrabsa.org

Southwest Florida
1801 Boy Scout Drive
Fort Myers, FL 33907
Phone: 941-936-8072
www.scoutswf.org

Southwest Georgia
930 West Oglethorpe Boulevard
Albany, GA 31701
Phone: 912-436-7226
members.surfsouth.com/
  ~swgacbsa

Southwest Michigan
1035 West Maple Street
Kalamazoo, MI 49008
Phone: 616-343-4687
www.bsaswmc.org

Stonewall Jackson Area
801 Hopeman Parkway
Waynesboro, VA 22980-0599
Phone: 540-943-6675
www.bsa-sjac.org

Suffolk County
7 Scouting Boulevard
Medford, NY 11763-2292
Phone: 631-924-7000
No website

Susquehanna
815 Northway Road
Williamsport, PA 17701-3891
Phone: 570-326-5121
No website

Suwannee River Area
2729 West Pensacola
Tallahassee, FL 32304
Phone: 850-576-4146
www.suwanneeriver.net

Tall Pine
507 West Atherton Road
Flint, MI 48507-2404
Phone: 810-235-2531
www.gfn.org/tpc

Tecumseh
326 South Thompson Avenue
Springfield, OH 45506
Phone: 937-325-6449
www.tecumsehcouncilbsa.org

Theodore Roosevelt
544 Broadway
Massapequa, NY 11758
Phone: 516-797-7600
www.trcbsa.org

Three Fires
415 North Second Street
St. Charles, IL 60174
Phone: 630-584-9250
www.threefirescouncil.org

Three Rivers
4650 Cardinal Drive
Beaumont, TX 77705
Phone: 409-842-5240
www.3rcbsa.com

Tidewater
1032 Heatherwood Drive
Virginia Beach, VA 23455
Phone: 757-497-2688
www.pilotonline.com/boyscouts

Trails West
1055 Harrison Avenue
Wood River, IL 62095
Phone: 618-259-2145
No website

Transatlantic
Unit 29242
APO AE 09102
Phone: 011-49-621-4877087
www.geocities.com/Yosemite/
  3525/transatlantic.html

Trapper Trails
1200 East 5400 South
Ogden, UT 84403-4599
Phone: 801-479-5460
www.trappertrails.org

Tri-State Area
733 Seventh Avenue
Huntington, WV 25701-2199
Phone: 304-523-3408
No website

Tukabatchee Area
3067 Carter Hill Road
Montgomery, AL 36111
Phone: 334-262-2697
No website

Tuscarora
316 East Walnut Street
Goldsboro, NC 27533-1436
Phone: 919-734-1714
No website

Twin Rivers
253 Washington Avenue,
    Extension
Albany, NY 12205
Phone: 518-869-6436
www.trc-bsa.org

Twin Valley
724 Madison Avenue
Mankato, MN 56001
Phone: 507-387-3123
No website

Utah National Parks
250 West 500 North
Provo, UT 84601
Phone: 801-373-4185
www.unpcbsa.org

Ventura County
509 Daily Drive
Camarillo, CA 93010-5820
Phone: 805-482-8938
www.vccbsa.org

Verdugo Hills
1325 Grandview Avenue
Glendale, CA 91201
Phone: 818-243-6282
www.vhcbsa.org

Viking
5300 Glenwood Avenue
Minneapolis, MN 55422
Phone: 763-545-4550
www.vikingbsa.org

Virgin Islands
1 Veterans Drive
St. Thomas, VI 00801-0175
Phone: 340-774-2752
No website

Voyageurs Area
3877 Stebner Road
Hermantown, MN 55811
Phone: 218-729-5811
www.vac-bsa.org

W.D. Boyce
614 NE Madison
Peoria, IL 61603
Phone: 309-673-6136
www.wdboyce.org

Wabash Valley
501 South 25th Street
Terre Haute, IN 47803-2603
Phone: 812-232-9496
www.wvcbsa.org

West Central Florida
11046 Johnson Boulevard
Seminole, FL 33772
Phone:727-391-3800
www.wcfcbsa.org

West Tennessee Area
1995 Hollywood Drive
Jackson, TN 38305
Phone: 901-668-3787
www.boyscouts.tn.org

Westark Area
1401 South 31st Street
Fort Smith, AR 72901
Phone: 501-782-7244
www.westarkbsa.org

Westchester-Putnam
41 Saw Mill River Road
Hawthorne, NY 10532
Phone: 914-773-1135
www.wpcbsa.org

Western Alaska
3117 Patterson Street
Anchorage, AK 99504-4041
Phone: 907-337-9547
No website

Western Colorado
839 Grand Avenue
Grand Junction, CO 81501
Phone: 970-243-0346
www.gj.net/post355

Western LA County
16525 Sherman Way, Suite C-8
Van Nuys, CA 91406-3753
Phone: 818-785-8700
www.bsa-la.org

Westmoreland-Fayette
2 Garden Center Drive
Greensburg, PA 15601
Phone: 724-837-1630
www.wfbsa.com

Will Rogers
412 South 14th Street
Ponca City, OK 74601
Phone: 580-765-6669
members.tripod.com/
    ~willrogerscouncil

Winnebago
2929 Airport Boulevard
Waterloo, IA 50703
Phone: 319-234-2867
www.winnebagobsa.org

Yankee Clipper
36 Amesbury Road
Haverhill, MA 01830-2802
Phone: 978-372-0791
Under construction

Yocona Area
505 Air Park Road
Tupelo, MS 38801
Phone: 662-842-2871
www.yocona.org

York Adams Area
2139 White Street
York, PA 17404-4940
Phone: 717-843-0901
www.yaac-bsa.org

Yucca
7601 Lockheed Drive
El Paso, TX 79925
Phone: 915-772-2292
No website

OA LODGE TO COUNCIL INDEX

OA LODGE TO COUNCIL INDEX

OA LODGE TO COUNCIL INDEX

INDEX

INDEX

WANTED!
COUNCIL PATCH WATCHERS

We are looking for Scouters in each Council to inform us when a new patch is being issued or when a merger occurs. This requires only a small effort and insures future volumes of this guide will have accurate information about your Council.

Attention Council Patch Watchers:
We need your help for the
2001 Jamboree Edition

Please help us complete the 2001 Jamboree Edition prior to the event by sending us your Council's 2001 National Jamboree Shoulder Patches (JSPs) and their stories as soon as possible. The first person to send us their Council's JSP and its story will receive a special Limited Edition S & E Jamboree Shoulder Patch as a thank you. Check our website to see which JSPs we have received, or send us an e-mail, fax, or letter.

We always invite readers that find errors in this book or have any additional information, comments, or suggestions to also contact us.

> e-mail: sd@scoutpatch.com
> Fax: 845-362-3252
> Phone: 888-CSP-BOOK

MAIL TO: S & E PUBLISHING COMPANY
5 Beaver Dam Road
Pomona, NY 10970

If you are interested, please copy this form and send it to us via e-mail (there is a form on-line), fax, or U. S. Postal Service, and we will send you a Patch Watcher Kit.

Date: _____

Name: _____

Address: _____

City: _____ State: _____ Zip: _____

Phone: _____ e-mail: _____

Council: _____ Rank: _____

Scouting Position: _____

Lodge: _____ Lodge #: _____

VISIT OUR WEBSITE AT: www.scoutpatch.com
e-mail: sd@scoutpatch.com

ORDERING INFORMATION

THE BOY SCOUT COUNCIL SHOULDER PATCH GUIDE, VOLUME FOUR is available at Council Scout Shops, Trading Posts, OA Lodges, Scouting distributors, and bookstores nationwide, or send a check or money order for $16.00 plus your local sales tax, and $4.00 for shipping and handling to:

> S & E PUBLISHING COMPANY
> Suite 104
> 5 Beaver Dam Road
> Pomona, NY 10970
> sd@scoutpatch.com

Volumes One, Two, and Three (also called the 1997, 1998, and 1999/Third Editions) are out-of-print, but a small quantity of each is still available. These are collector's items, so order quickly before they are gone.

THE BOY SCOUT COUNCIL SHOULDER PATCH GUIDE is a continually evolving publication with each Volume containing 50 or more different patches, and new and updated information. It is our practice to retire both patches that have changed and patches from Councils that have merged since our last volume. You may see and learn about all the regular issue CSPs that have been in use since 1997 by purchasing the complete set of Guides.

Name: _____

Address:_____

City: _____ State: _____ Zip: _____

Phone: _____ e-mail: _____

Council: _____ Date: _____

Quantity	Description	Cost	Amount
_____	THE BOY SCOUT COUNCIL SHOULDER PATCH GUIDE VOLUME THREE (also called 1999/THIRD EDITION)	$20.00	_____
_____	THE BOY SCOUT COUNCIL SHOULDER PATCH GUIDE VOLUME TWO (also called 1998 EDITION)	$20.00	_____
_____	THE BOY SCOUT COUNCIL SHOULDER PATCH GUIDE VOLUME ONE (also called 1997 EDITION)	$20.00	_____
_____	S & E Logo T-Shirt Circle one: `Adult LG, XLG, or XXLG	$18.00	_____
_____	S & E Logo Baseball Cap	$20.00	_____

Shipping and Handling: S & H _____
($4.00 for one item and $1.00 for each additional item)
Please add your local sales tax.   Sales Tax: _____

TOTAL COST _____

NOTES

VISIT OUR WEBSITE AT: www.scoutpatch.com
e-mail: sd@scoutpatch.com